THE ART OF
PAINTING

Step-by-step instruction and demonstration
in color mixing and painting techniques
selected from The Grumbacher Library.

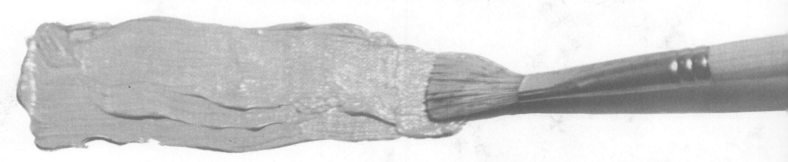

Edited by Walter Brooks

GOLDEN PRESS · *New York*

CONTENTS

To supplement the text and provide quicker reference we include here a brief glossary.

ACCENT: Emphasis in a part of the design or composition, a sharp detail.

ACHROMATIC: Black, white and grays. Work executed without color.

ACRYLIC POLYMER (POLYMER): A generic term for all synthetic resin paints (plastic), mediums and materials for artists' use.

CAST SHADOW: The dark area that results when an object or form interrupts a source of light.

CHROMA: The relative hue intensity of a color.

COMPOSITION: The arrangement of the various elements in a drawing or painting.

DRY BRUSH: A technique employing a brush with very little water to achieve a broken color effect.

FIXATIVE: A colorless coating used to spray on drawings to prevent smearing. It can be applied by mouth atomizer and is also available in pressurized cans. (Tuffilm Spray)

FORM: The structure or design of an object or work of art.

GLAZE: Color thinned to a transparent state and applied over previously painted areas to modify the original color. (See also Underpainting)

GOUACHE: (Tempera) Opaque watercolors and the technique of painting with such colors using white to make tints.

HIGHLIGHT: Those small areas on a painting or drawing on which light is the brightest.

HUE: That attribute which distinguishes color by name, i.e. red, blue, etc.

IMPASTO: A manner of painting in which the paint is laid on thickly so that texture stands out in relief.

MEDIUM: The material used for a drawing or painting, i.e. Oils, Watercolors, Pastels, etc. Any substance added to color to facilitate application or to achieve a desired effect.

SHADE: Color made darker by the addition of black.

SPLIT HAIR TECHNIQUE: Pressure applied near the ferrule of the brush causing the hairs at the tip of the brush to spread out. This can also be achieved by rubbing the brush across paper until the hairs are spread.

STUDY: A detailed drawing or painting of an element to be incorporated into a finished work.

THUMBNAIL: A small, rough sketch used to plan composition before starting the finished drawing.

TINT: Color made lighter by the addition of white. The result of applying a wash or glaze over a white surface.

UNDERPAINTING: Preliminary painting used as a base for subsequent glazes, or to achieve a textured base for subsequent painting not possible by direct application of color. (See glaze)

VALUE: Relative lightness and darkness. The relation of one part of a picture to another with respect to lightness and darkness.

VIGNETTE: A drawing or painting which is shaded to a soft edge.

WASH: A highly fluid application of color.

Designed and edited by Walter Brooks
Copyright© 1968 by M. Grumbacher, Inc.
460 West 34th Street, New York, N.Y.
All rights reserved.

Library of Congress Catalog Card Number 68-29675
Produced by Western Publishing Company, Inc.
Printed in U.S.A.

INTRODUCTION

The basic urge to express oneself, record surroundings, tell a story, is one that will out—with or without training. Evidence of this can be seen in cave drawings and the very expressive primitive art which is a part of every country and ethnic group. History shows us convincingly, however, that the masters of art have been those who became students of art. Those who, by study and exploration, expanded their capacity for expression. The act of painting becomes the art of painting by the combination of study, experience, and experiment. Painting exists and thrives as an art because the disciplines necessary to the act—expand rather than restrict its scope.

In *The Art of Painting* we attempt to provide the necessary balance between practical knowledge of tools, materials, mediums, surfaces, etc., and a visual inspiration to sustain the initial momentum and excitement of the determined student.

It is difficult to express visual sensation in verbal terms, or to describe completely all of the instinctive personal factors that become a part of the painting process. In this book, artists demonstrate step by step their procedures for producing a painting. The value of such instruction can be increased by the degree to which the student is stimulated to the act of painting—not only by the examples shown but by following the direction suggested for personal exploration and growth.

Filbert   F

MATERIALS

Oil colors are the most satisfying medium for the beginner. With simple instruction it is possible to develop a degree of confidence that can sustain the initial enthusiasm for painting. For this reason we have started with, and devoted the major portion of the book to this medium.

The section on color mixing, which applies in theory to all media, is discussed in this book in terms of oil because of their facility for demonstration and instruction. Oil paints lend themselves to the study of color theory and color mixing because they do not change appreciably in color from the wet to the dry state and, also, because mixtures can be adjusted without concern that the paints will become dry on the palette before a desired result is achieved.

The studio or work area should be adequately lighted. North light is the most desirable because it is so constant, but is not absolutely necessary. Before painting under artificial light some time should be spent studying the optical effects that fluorescent and incandescent light have on various colors. Much preparatory work can be done at night — but if at all possible painting should be done during daylight hours.

The area should be arranged so that there is room to step back and view the painting as it progresses. When painting in oils, most artists prefer to work from a standing position so that they can move back and by constantly viewing the over-all painting, avoid overworking any

one particular area at the expense of the entire work. This generally makes for a more direct and vigorous approach. The painting should be adequately braced when it is being worked on. To this end, budget permitting, a fairly substantial vertical easel is a valuable piece of equipment in the studio. It can be raised or lowered for proper working height and can be tilted to avoid glare on the canvas. A small table next to the easel will serve to hold the palette, brushes, and colors when painting.

Brushes are many and varied. The bulk of painting in oil is done with bristle brushes, and it is best for the beginner to stay with these. Sables (soft hair brushes) are excellent painting tools but when not properly used, or overused, they have a tendency to make your work slick or fussy.

Turpentine, or an improved paint thinner, Grumtine, should be used to clean brushes, the palette, or mixed with linseed oil as a painting medium. Do not use the thinner excessively as a medium by itself since it tends to dilute the binder resulting in colors which may dust off when dry. A popular medium for oil painting is a mixture of turpentine and linseed oil in equal amounts.

The artists represented in this book, in the discussion of their palettes include colors not on the basic list which follows. You might want to add some of these other colors after you have confidence with this recommended list.

]

COLORS:
    Zinc Yellow (Lemon Yellow)
    Cadmium Yellow, Medium
    Cadmium Red, Light
    Alizarin Crimson
    French Ultramarine Blue
    Thalo® Blue
    Yellow Ochre
    Burnt Sienna
    Burnt Umber
    Thalo Green
    Superba White

BRUSHES: (The brush style is designated by a letter following the series number.) This list will meet basic needs.
    F — Flats (flat, square-edge, long bristle) #2, #6, #10
    B — Brights (flat, square-edge, short bristle) #4, #8
    R — Rounds (round, pointed bristle) #6, sable #4
    L — Longs (flat, square-edge, long sable) #10
    Filberts — (flat, oval edge, long bristle) #4, #8

CANVAS: Fabrics prepared for painting. Available as panel, stretched on frames, or by the yard.

PAINTING KNIFE: A trowel-type flexible knife in a variety of shapes and sizes.

PALETTE: Wood, plastic, or disposable paper. A color mixing area. Also a personal selection of colors.

PALETTE KNIFE: For scraping palette clean and mixing colors. Can be used as a painting knife.

OIL CUP: Containers which can be clipped to the palette — one cup for the medium, the other for brush cleaner.

TURPENTINE (or Grumtine): For cleaning equipment and thinning mediums.

LINSEED OIL: The traditional "binder" for oil colors. Also used as a medium.

CHARCOAL: Either pencils or sticks. For preliminary sketching on canvas.

FIXATIVE SPRAY: For fixing charcoal drawing on canvas before painting. Available in spray cans (Tuffilm Spray) or for use with mouth atomizer.

PAINT BOX: A desirable piece of equipment for storing brushes, paint, palette, and accessories when painting outdoors.

EASEL: A support for the canvas during painting. Available as collapsible tripod, studio types and as combination sketch box units. In some sketch boxes the lids serve as easels.

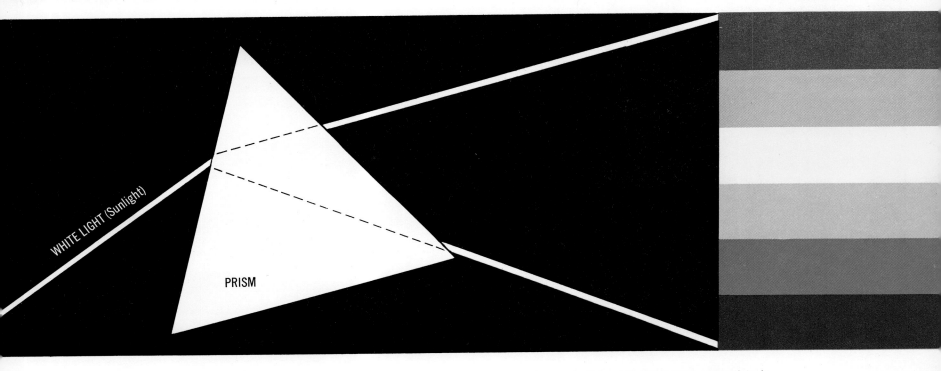

All color is contained in white light. When white light is passed through a crystal prism, it is dispersed into the spectrum range of visible colors. It also can be reestablished as white light.

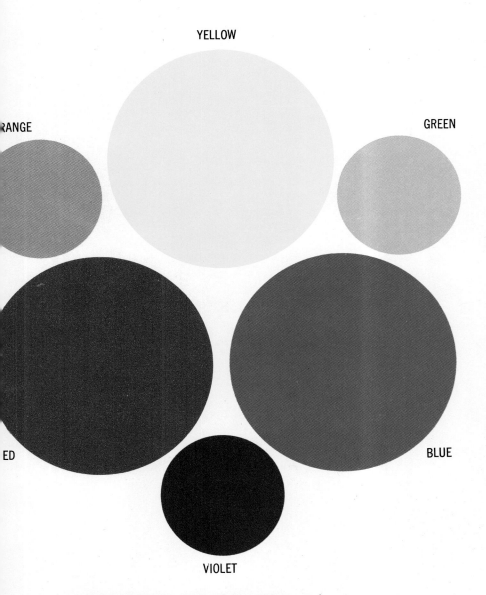

In paint mixing, the entire range of the spectrum can be produced by the selective use of three primary colors: Red, Yellow and Blue. Unlike the **light spectrum,** which results in white light when all of its components are mixed, the **pigment spectrum** produces a dark value approximating black.

COLOR THEORY

BASIC COLOR PRINCIPLES

All Color Theory is based on the principle that *color is light*. Normally, all of the colors we see are contained in the light reflected by pigments which, as chemical compounds, have the property of selectivity absorbing certain colors of the light spectrum. Thus, an object producing the visual sensation of *red* contains pigmentation which absorbs all of the colored rays of white light except the *red* which it reflects. *White* pigment absorbs none of the colored rays . . . while *black* absorbs all of the colors of the spectrum.

The nature of the illumination with which we work affects the colors we see. Natural light is not constant and the color bands of the spectrum are affected by the position of the sun due to the seasons of the year, the time of day and atmospheric conditions. Artificial light affects the appearance of colors because the spectrum range of each type of artificial light is determined by the physical nature of the light source (fluorescent, incandescent, etc.).

As an illustration of this phenomenon, examine simultaneously two paint-outs of an identical color: one under fluorescent, and the other under incandescent light. Notice the obvious difference.

This very elementary knowledge of what color is accepted to be is all that we, as painters, need to know about the physics of color.

(continued on page 8)

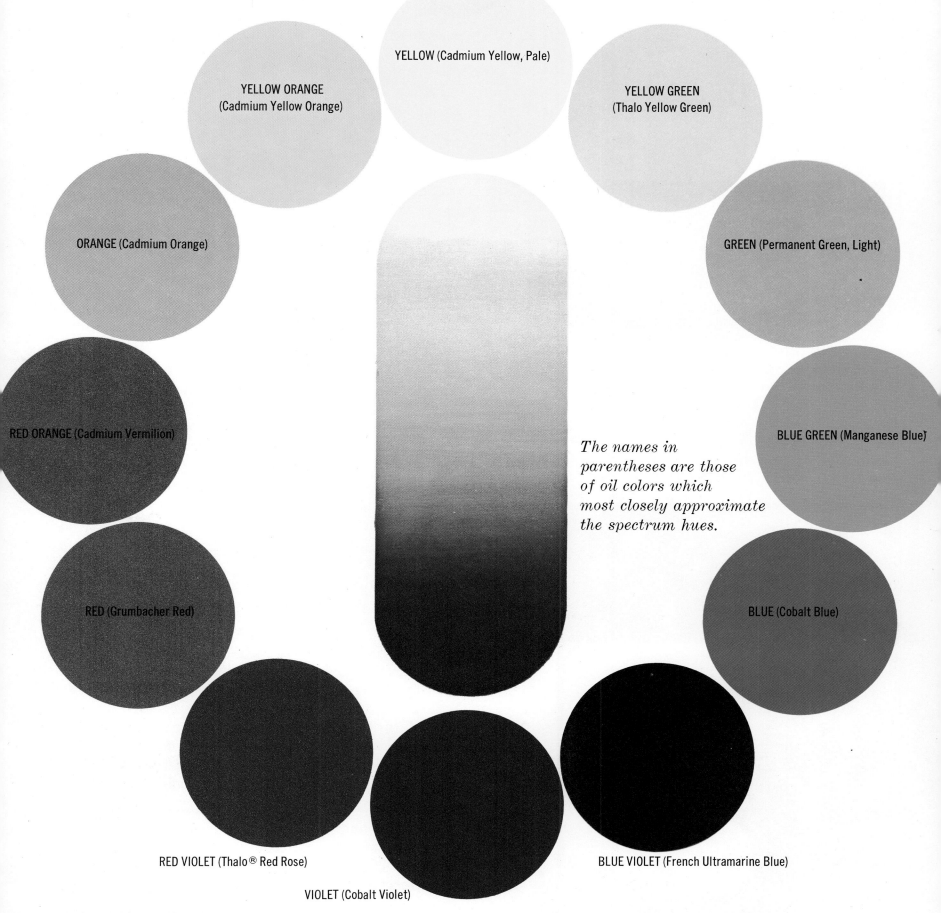

YELLOW (Cadmium Yellow, Pale)

YELLOW ORANGE
(Cadmium Yellow Orange)

YELLOW GREEN
(Thalo Yellow Green)

ORANGE (Cadmium Orange)

GREEN (Permanent Green, Light)

The names in parentheses are those of oil colors which most closely approximate the spectrum hues.

RED ORANGE (Cadmium Vermilion)

BLUE GREEN (Manganese Blue)

RED (Grumbacher Red)

BLUE (Cobalt Blue)

RED VIOLET (Thalo® Red Rose)

BLUE VIOLET (French Ultramarine Blue)

VIOLET (Cobalt Violet)

THREE PRIMARY COLORS SYSTEM

The simplest and most widely accepted method of applying color theory to painting is by means of the **Three Primary Colors System.**

A Color Wheel is an effective way of demonstrating this system. All the principal and intermediate hues of the light spectrum are represented on the Wheel by a series of 11 equidistant segments formed into a continuous band of 12 by the addition of Red Violet, which is missing from the light spectrum.

PRIMARY COLORS The three Primary Colors are: Red, Yellow and Blue.
SECONDARY COLORS The three Secondary Colors are: Orange, Violet, Green. Each is midway between the Primaries from which it can be mixed.
INTERMEDIATE COLORS The remaining colors are intermediates obtained by mixing adjoining Primary and Secondary Colors.
TERTIARY COLORS These represent a mixture of Secondary Colors.

The effect of background on an **achromatic value** can be seen in A. This effect is also true with color values. In contrast with black, the curved line of gray gives the impression of being lighter than against white.

Although each value in B is all of one tone, the illusion of gradation of value at the edges is the result of contrast with the adjacent values.

The heightening of contrast in C gives the effect of the center circle being whiter than the surrounding white of the paper.

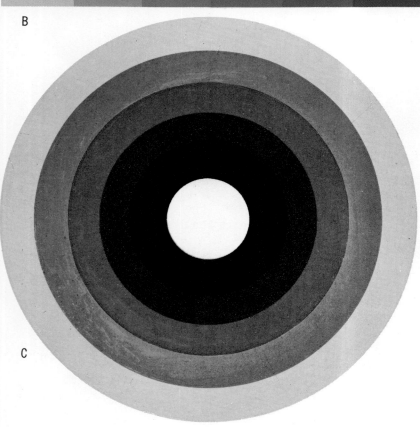

THE THREE DIMENSIONS OF COLOR

If we were to ask someone who has had little or no instruction in color theory to describe the difference between three colors: an intense Red, a dull Red, and a Yellow . . . his first reaction would undoubtedly be . . . "One color is Yellow and the other two are Reds." He might then further indicate that one of the two Reds is duller than the other. Finally, he might conclude that the Yellow is lighter than the Reds.

This layman's analysis describes, in the simplest terms, the three distinctly different and measurable characteristics of all colors, which are commonly known as the *Three Dimensions of Color.*

HUE . . . This is the most characteristic dimension which identifies a color by name, i.e., Red, Yellow, Blue, Blue Green, etc. Every color falls into a definite Hue category when related to the spectrum range of colors.

INTENSITY (also called *CHROMA*) . . . This dimension represents the relative intensity of hue. Colors of greater hue saturation can be described as being of higher Intensity than duller colors of the same hue dimension. For example, Burnt Sienna which the layman might describe as a Brown, is actually a relatively low intensity reddish Orange hue.

VALUE . . . This dimension represents the brightness of illumination and, under normal lighting conditions, locates a color's position in relation to a scale of grays between White and Black. A color such as an intense Yellow is light or high in value. An intense Violet is dark or low in value.

EACH OF THE THREE DIMENSIONS OF COLOR HAS A DEFINITE APPLICATION IN PAINTING.

Hue is important to the artist because of its psychological impact on the viewer. Moods of a picture may be emphasized by the selection of an appropriate range of hues. Yellows and Orange, associated with sunshine and warmth, are considered cheerful colors. Red, associated with fire, blood, etc., is usually thought of as a violent and exciting color. Blue, a cool color, connotes serenity, while Green implies restfulness and Violet is mysterious.

Normally, hues such as Red and Yellow are regarded as being *warm* and hues such as Blue and Blue Green are *cool*. This is a general color temperature classification, Although Thalo Red Rose is a warm color, it is cool when compared to Cadmium Vermilion.

Warm colors appear warmer and the cools seem cooler when contrasted with their opposites in temperature.

Warm colors tend to advance while cool colors seem to recede on the painted surface.

Intensity . . . This dimension is important because within a hue the artist can simulate depth and emphasize contrasts through variations in intensity.

In nature, under uniform lighting conditions, a color in the foreground will always appear more intense than the same color in the distance. The painter can also force colors to recede by reducing their intensity. A color will appear *more* intense when placed on or near a duller color of the same hue.

Value is the only dimension of color which can exist outside of color and is so represented by the scale of achromatic grays on page 10. Value is probably the most important dimension for the artist seeking to simulate form and effect emphasis through contrasts in light and shade.

The value of any color can be made lighter (*Tints*) by the addition of White or by means of a lighter color of the same hue. Colors which are made darker in value by the addition of a darker color of the same hue or by mixture with Black are called *Shades*. Both tints and shades, which represent distinct changes in the value dimension of a color, also tend to reduce the intensity and, in many instances, also effect its hue.

The painter should determine his lightest and darkest values and paint within this range. Light colors appear lighter against dark backgrounds and vice versa.

COLOR MIXING

Color mixing can *only* be learned through practical application and experimentation but a knowledge of color theory will give the beginner a basis for such application and experimentation.

To illustrate a problem in color mixing and its solution, let us assume that we are limited to a palette of three colors: Cadmium Yellow, Pale; Grumbacher Red and Cobalt Blue, plus Ivory Black and Zinc White. From this Primary selection, we are required to mix an Olive Green. As every color can be analyzed as to its relative Hue, Intensity and Value, Olive Green might be described as basically a *Yellow Green hue* of moderately *low intensity* and of approximately *middle value*. Our first step, therefore, in mixing this color is to blend the Blue and Yellow to produce a basic Yellow Green. This mixture results in a color of relatively high intensity. To reduce this intensity (*neutralize* this color), we have two choices:

A. We can add Red, the complement of Green, until the desired reduction of intensity is achieved (adjusting it with additional Blue, if necessary, because the true complement of Yellow Green is Red Violet). The resultant mixture may be too dark because as the intensity of a color is diminished by complementary mixture, its value is also lowered. Therefore, White may be required to adjust this dimension.

B. The alternate solution to this problem is to utilize a Gray, mixed from the Black and White, to reduce the intensity of the basic Yellow Green. Gray, employed to lower the intensity of any color, will not darken that color (unlike complementary mixtures), if it has the same value as the color.   *(continued on page 12)*

A

B

C

In the simple studies above can be seen some effects of value, intensity, and hue in painting. "A" is a high key arrangement with a close value range. The intensity is quite high in this analagous color scheme.

"B" is a middle value arrangement. The only intense color is the cold blue in this split-complementary scheme. "C" employs a wider value range, as well as greater variations in color temperature and color intensities. Notice how the warmer and more intense color areas appear to come to the fore.

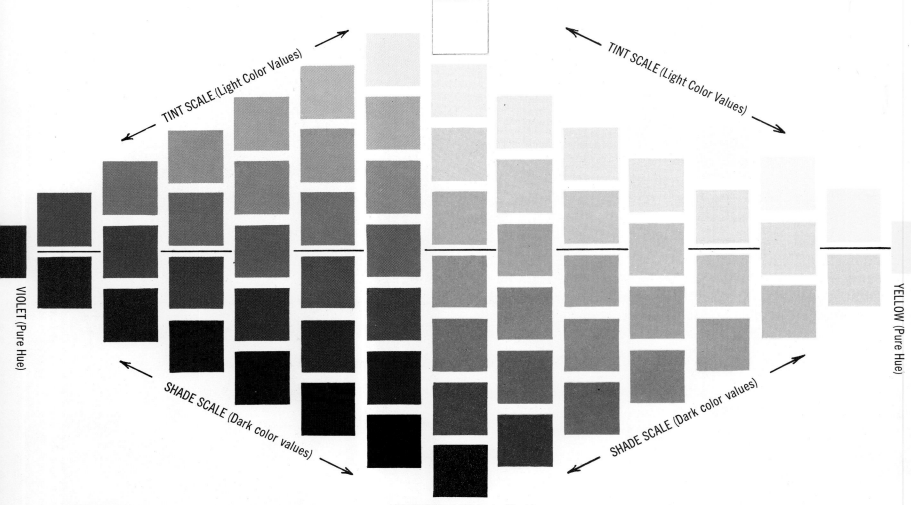

TINT SCALE (Light Color Values)

TINT SCALE (Light Color Values)

VIOLET (Pure Hue)

YELLOW (Pure Hue)

SHADE SCALE (Dark color values)

SHADE SCALE (Dark color values)

VALUE SCALE (White to Black)

The complements (Violet and Yellow) are shown at the ends of this diagram. The central line represents a **direct progression of complementary mixtures.** This is also demonstrated in the color wheel on page 7, showing the result of a mixture of the complements Yellow and Violet. Balanced color complements neutralize each other and produce gray or values approaching black. The achro-

matic **value scale** from white to black is in the center of the diagram. The **tint scale** (the upper diagonals of color) is white mixed with the pure color. The **shade scale** (lower diagonals) has black added to the pure color. The **intermediate steps** are the result of complementary mixtures tinted with white and shaded with black.

FULL STRENGTH COLORS

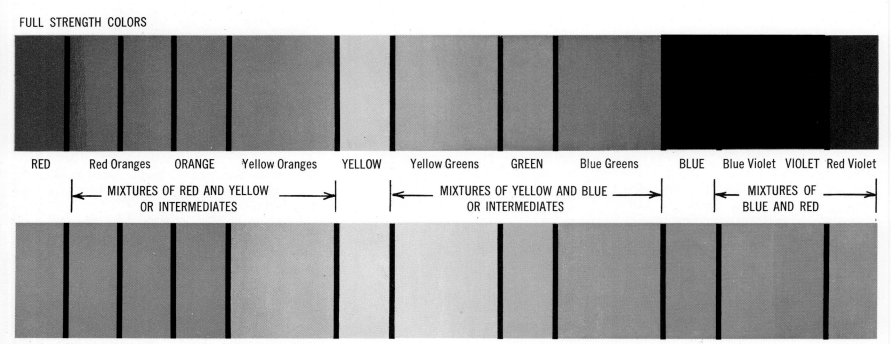

| RED | Red Oranges | ORANGE | Yellow Oranges | YELLOW | Yellow Greens | GREEN | Blue Greens | BLUE | Blue Violet | VIOLET | Red Violet |

← MIXTURES OF RED AND YELLOW OR INTERMEDIATES → ← MIXTURES OF YELLOW AND BLUE OR INTERMEDIATES → ← MIXTURES OF BLUE AND RED →

TINTS (HIGHER VALUES) White added to full strength colors.

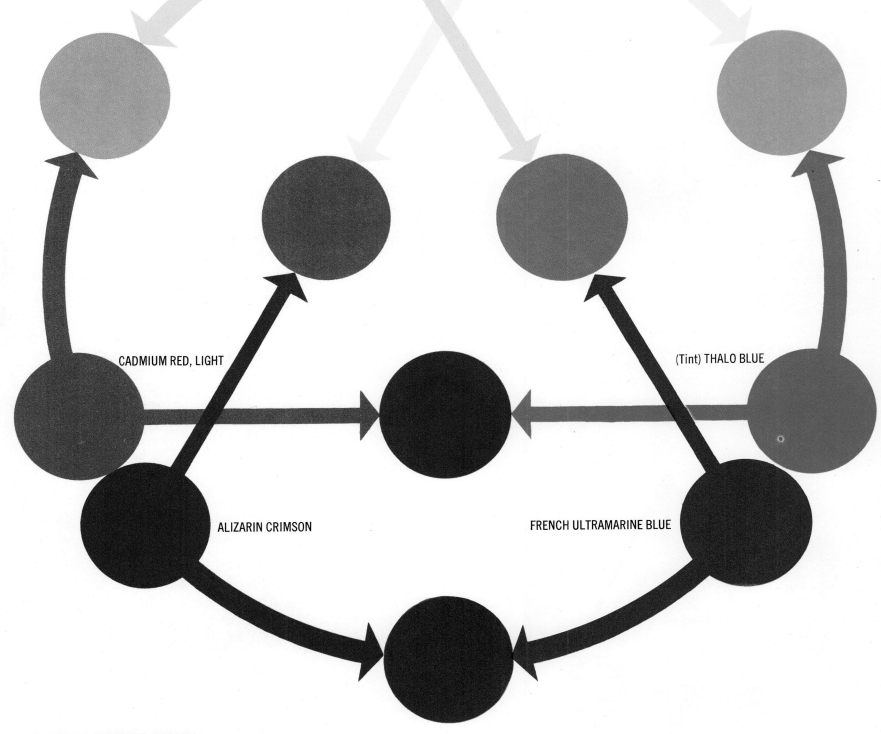

CADMIUM YELLOW, MEDIUM

ZINC YELLOW (Lemon Yellow)

CADMIUM RED, LIGHT

(Tint) THALO BLUE

ALIZARIN CRIMSON

FRENCH ULTRAMARINE BLUE

THE DOUBLE PRIMARIES PALETTE

By selecting **two colors** for each of the three primary hue divisions of the spectrum, the degree of intensity of secondary mixtures can be controlled with much greater accuracy. For example, Thalo Blue and Lemon Yellow produce a variety of relatively intense greens. A second primary blue, French Ultramarine Blue, when mixed with Lemon Yellow produces progressively less intense greens, and this same French Ultramarine Blue when mixed with the second primary yellow, Cadmium Yellow, Medium produces a variety of greens which are still further reduced in intensity. This selective cross-combination of mixtures works just as effectively in all areas of the double-primaries palette.

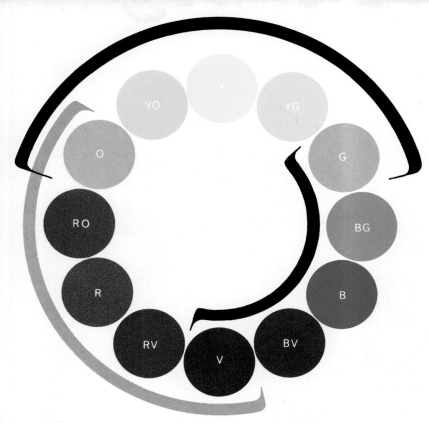

This diagram depicts an arbitrary selection of analogous colors, each group consisting of five colors balanced on a Primary. Analogous groupings can be selected from any segment of the circle and can be limited to as few as two colors.

The arrows in the diagram below indicate direct complements.
The shaded triangle indicates a split-complementary group.
The open triangle indicates a triadic harmony group.
The pointer can be rotated to any position on the circle and will locate similar color relationships.

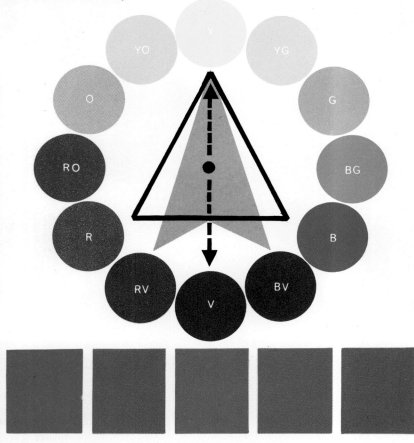

In this chart, Cobalt Blue has been reduced in intensity while value is maintained by the addition of Black and White. High intensity colors appear to advance and low intensity colors to recede.

(continued from page 9)

Artists' colors are produced in an extensive range of hues and intensities. The painter can readily select a palette of colors appropriate for any subject and thus, radically reduce the time and effort involved in color mixing.

The palette diagrammed on page 11 is an excellent selection for experimentation in color mixing. Study this carefully and test the various mixtures illustrated. Make your own tests with other combinations. Compare the tints produced by transparent applications on a white background and those, of equal value, made with the addition of White. Note the variations in the physical properties of each color, such as its tinting strength and degree of opacity or transparency.

It is impossible to judge accurately a color in isolation. A mixture which appears correct on the palette may not be so in relation to other colors when it is applied.

COLOR HARMONY

The mind normally attempts to equalize or neutralize the effect of extremes in stimuli because exposure to such extremes is disturbing. It is for this reason that the exercise of moderation is considered the keynote to harmony for all sensory perception.

Moderation can, however, become monotonous if the spice of variety is lacking. Accents of relatively acute extremes introduced into moderate diets of color, food, sound, odor or texture arouse and maintain interest.

There are three methods which may be used, *either separately or in combination*, to produce Color Harmony:

MONOCHROMATIC Harmony arrived at by utilizing one color plus White and Black. Certain subjects lend themselves to this color scheme. It is a challenging exercise that relies for effect upon the value and intensity ranges of a single hue within a painting.

COMPLEMENTARY Direct, Split-Complementary and *Triadic harmonies* represent relationships in color through the participation of all of the three Primaries in comparatively uniform visual distribution *(see diagram)*. However, it is suggested that in no combination should *all* of the colors be represented as fully intense. This is in accordance with the principle of moderation, because the three fully intense Primary Colors present in any such combinations actually represent the *extreme* condensation of the complete spectrum range. Thus, an intense Red Orange flower arrangement can be extremely effective against a pale Blue Green background which is relatively low in intensity. Should the Blue Green be too strong in hue, there would be a struggle for dominance with the Red Orange. The result might be somewhat discordant and disturbing.

When using complementary color schemes, handle them with restraint until you become more familiar with color.

ANALOGOUS (see diagram on page 12) These color harmonies are somewhat muted since only two of the three Primary colors are present in some combinations. In those instances where all three are present, two of them are in relatively weak concentrations. For example, at the Yellow segment of the color wheel, we might select an analogous grouping of Orange (*Yellow* + Red); Yellow Orange (*Yellow* + Red); Yellow; Yellow Green (*Yellow* + Blue) and Green (*Yellow* + Blue). By making one hue dominant in the painting . . . *Yellow* in this instance . . . and using adjacent colors with it, a pleasing balance can be maintained.

As an exercise in discovering the potentials of all of these color schemes, start by making abstract thumbnails. Without undue concern for drawing or form, use monochromatic, complementary and analogous harmonies alone or in combination. This can give you a feeling for the value and color range necessary for harmonious effects. You will discover that the relationship between color areas of high or low intensity, as well as the value range within the painting are the keys to the success of any scheme.

COLOR MIXING

The demonstrations through page 21 were prepared by Victor Kalin, noted painter and illustrator, who discusses technique as well as color in connection with still life and flowers.

In this painting are combined a number of popular, yet difficult objects for the student. Metals and glass offer the problems of texture with their sparkling well-defined highlights and elusive reflected colors. Apples, always a favorite subject, offer a challenge in the proper indication of subtle color and highlights within the form.

As shown in Step 1, the composition was sketched on the canvas with a little Yellow Ochre, thinned with turpentine. In Step 2, elements of the painting were then blocked in covering the canvas with areas of color as quickly as possible. The main reason for this is that a color may look correct against the background of white canvas, and can be completely out of key when neighboring colors are painted in. This process of color balancing is much easier in the early stages while the elements are merely blocked-in shapes and it is relatively easy to scrape off a color and replace it with another. (continued on page 14)

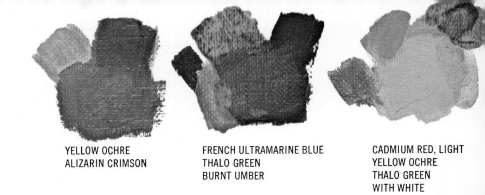

YELLOW OCHRE
ALIZARIN CRIMSON

FRENCH ULTRAMARINE BLUE
THALO GREEN
BURNT UMBER

CADMIUM RED, LIGHT
YELLOW OCHRE
THALO GREEN
WITH WHITE

The background was kept simple with subtle color changes within it for interest. Values were kept fairly light with no strong colors so that this area could act as a foil for the stronger, more chromatic colors and deeper play of value in the objects.

The drapery and copper container were painted as though there was nothing in front of them. The pitcher, because it is transparent, consists of little more than a few highlights and shadows to suggest its form. It is this subtle relationship between crisp highlights and darks that gives a painting of glass the qualities that suggest the brittle, shiny hardness of the material.

For the brass candlestick which presents the problem of painting a shiny metallic surface, Lemon Yellow and Burnt Umber were used in varying mixtures with Burnt Sienna for the warm color reflections on the side next to the large bronze bowl. The effect of brilliance in the candlestick is achieved by limited touches of very intense Lemon Yellow at the edge of the highlights.

It is interesting to note that although apples are usually thought of as being bright red, very little intense red is applied and in reality nearly all the colors found in the fruit are the result of mixtures of Yellow Ochre with Alizarin Crimson; Cadmium Red, Light; Yellow Ochre and Thalo Green.

When mixing colors to obtain a light tint, start with a quantity of white and add colors to it until you have the value you want. With darker or more intense colors, start with the color that is to be most dominant in the mixture and add color to this until you reach the mixture you want. Certain colors, you will find, are very powerful — a little goes a long way. Thalo Blue and Thalo Green are in this category. Test all of your colors by mixing small quantities with white and with each other to get a feeling for amounts needed in any mixture.

The mixtures above show combinations used to obtain some of the colors in the painting. For lighter, less intense tints, white was added to these colors.

YELLOW OCHRE
FRENCH ULTRAMARINE BLUE
BURNT UMBER
WITH WHITE

LEMON YELLOW
BURNT UMBER

THALO GREEN
YELLOW OCHRE
BURNT SIENNA
BURNT UMBER

BURNT SIENNA
FRENCH ULTRAMARINE BLUE

THALO GREEN
BURNT UMBER
WITH A TOUCH
OF WHITE

In painting a white object, the subtle play of value and color can be influenced by any number of conditions including: form, texture (dull or glossy—rough or smooth), color from the light source, and color reflected from surrounding objects. If you examine closely the colors reflected in a white china cup, you will discover that it catches light from several different sources, such as a window, an uncovered incandescent bulb or possibly a tinted lamp shade. It must, in reality, be lower in value than white in order to have the light areas appear sufficiently light. Even the highlights are not pure white, for they also contain some coloration from the light sources; the blue of the sky, or the warm tones of the electric light.

On the left can be seen the stages of laying in color for the painting on page 17. This subject deals with the problem of painting a white object.

In Step 1, the composition is sketched on the canvas using French Ultramarine Blue thinned with turpentine. In Step 2, color is blocked in on all areas of the canvas so that colors can be adjusted and balanced to each other as the painting develops.

In Step 3, the areas of the canvas have been blocked in and detail started in portions of the painting.

The pitcher was painted with an over-all color using French Ultramarine Blue, Burnt Sienna, and White. The jar, slightly warmer, was French Ultramarine Blue, Yellow Ochre, and White.

As can be seen in step three and in the finished painting, the background was kept just below middle value to contrast with the white pitcher and jar. Both containers reflect the blue of the background drapery and the color of the lemons is reflected in the pitcher. In this analogous color scheme, the background color is more intense than both jar and pitcher but not so strong as to detract from the strong chromatic accents of the lemons and limes. The deep value in the jar also helps to accent the color of the fruit. Highlights were put in last in a manner that indicated the form of the object.

THALO GREEN
FRENCH ULTRAMARINE BLUE
YELLOW OCHRE WITH WHITE

YELLOW OCHRE
FRENCH ULTRAMARINE BLUE
WITH WHITE

YELLOW OCHRE
THALO GREEN
CADMIUM YELLOW, PALE

YELLOW OCHRE
CADMIUM YELLOW, PALE
FRENCH ULTRAMARINE BLUE

BURNT SIENNA
FRENCH ULTRAMARINE BLUE
WITH WHITE

BURNT SIENNA
FRENCH ULTRAMARINE BLU
WITH WHITE

The physical act of mixing paint, applying it to the canvas, building surface texture, and blending and fusing colors can be an exciting experience that sometimes supersedes realism in the finished painting.

The freedom a painting knife offers for the application of color can be an interesting change from the brush; also, glazes can be applied to dry areas of paint with a piece of cotton rag and colors mixed and blended on the canvas with finger or thumb. Only the imagination of the painter limits the approach, restricts his technique, or dictates materials.

In the painting of roses on page 19, the flowers are part of an over-all composition of colors and textures rather than a specifically featured element of the painting.

In Step 1, the drawing was sketched on the canvas using Yellow Ochre thinned with turpentine. Then Step 2, color was blocked in on the over-all painting and, as the painting progressed, the possibilities for exciting textural effects in the background became more evident. As a result, the over-all surface texture gained in importance and in the finished painting the flowers were no longer as dominant as in the original conception.

The background is a subtle blending of colors used in the flowers and leaves kept low in intensity and value in order to accent the roses.

Note that in this and the preceding painting the most intense colors are restricted to a small portion of the painting. In the painting of the pitcher and jar it is the lemon and limes, and in this flower study, the color in the blossoms.

ALIZARIN CRIMSON
CADMIUM YELLOW, MEDIUM
WITH WHITE

CADMIUM YELLOW, MEDIUM
CADMIUM RED, LIGHT
YELLOW OCHRE

YELLOW OCHRE
THALO GREEN
ALIZARIN CRIMSON

BURNT UMBER
THALO GREEN

FRENCH ULTRAMARINE BLUE
BURNT UMBER
WITH WHITE

YELLOW OCHRE
BURNT UMBER
WITH WHITE

Flower painting gives the artist the opportunity of using his colors in happy profusion. Cadmium Yellows, Oranges, and Reds give such flowers as Zinnias and Marigolds their hot, robust flavor while greens, blues, and Alizarin Crimson help handle the cooler tones of the Asters, Iris, and Lilacs. When painting flowers, pay attention to the over-all shape of the blossom and the definite pattern of its shadow. This is what gives each flower its distinctive shape and individual characteristics. In this painting, the light source is above and behind the subject and as a result almost all of the bouquet is in shadow. This makes an interesting study because the manner in which color is used must suggest the luminosity of the flowers and also indicate shadow areas. This subtle relationship

THALO GREEN
CADMIUM YELLOW, PALE
FRENCH ULTRAMARINE BLUE
WITH WHITE

is accomplished where the lighted areas blend into the shadow. It is here that the purest, brightest colors are used and these small touches suggest the over-all brightness of the subject. Likewise, the brass bowl gets its metallic characteristics by reflected light in the shadow area.

THALO GREEN
CADMIUM YELLOW, PALE
CADMIUM ORANGE

COBALT BLUE
YELLOW OCHRE
WITH WHITE

CADMIUM YELLOW, DEEP
ALIZARIN CRIMSON
WITH WHITE

THALO GREEN
ALIZARIN CRIMSON
CADMIUM YELLOW, MEDIUM

YELLOW OCHRE
FRENCH ULTRAMARINE BLUE
THALO GREEN
WITH WHITE

On the left is shown the preliminary lay-in of color. Within the essentially analogous color scheme of the finished painting, it has been possible to inject accents of pink and deeper red without disturbing the over-all effect. This works because the greatest area of the painting uses a basic color scheme and these accents are handled subtly.

The following demonstrations were prepared by Albert John Pucci, noted teacher and painter. Mr. Pucci, in his landscape painting, prefers to sketch and gather color notes on the spot and use them as a basis for painting in the studio.

In the preliminary step to the full color painting on pages 24-25 (shown below), the entire canvas was covered with a middle value mixture of Thalo Blue, Raw Umber, and Superba White. No attempt was made to put this down as a flat color, it was instead applied quite freely with the painting knife and spots where colors didn't mix too thoroughly were purposely allowed to remain. The overall texture and interest in this somewhat uneven underpainting made for intriguing effects when local color was applied over it.

In the **detail** above can be seen the freedom with which the brush and knife are used in applying color and the manner in which it is possible to take advantage of the exciting accidental effects of working over the rough ground color.

When the underpainting was dry, a round sable brush was used to sketch in the composition with a mixture of Thalo Blue and Raw Umber thinned with turpentine. After this, lighter areas were put in broadly with the painting knife. The underpainting color was allowed to come through where the knife hit only the high spots of the rough surface.

The distant trees and hills were put in with a bristle brush. Brushing color lightly with a bristle brush over this ground color can create diversified effects and indicate texture of trees, snow, and rocks. The dark shape of the barn was painted in the same color and value as the dark tree forms around and behind it. The warmer color accents in the barn and rocks were put in last.

SUPERBA WHITE WITH A
TOUCH OF THALO BLUE
AND RAW UMBER

THALO BLUE, WHITE AND A SPOT
OF FRENCH ULTRAMARINE BLUE

CADMIUM ORANGE AND
BURNT SIENNA

This basically analogous color scheme uses blues and greens predominantly with complementary accents of Cadmium Orange and Burnt Sienna.

12

WHITE WITH A TOUCH OF
THALO BLUE AND THALO GREEN

ALIZARIN CRIMSON,
THALO GREEN AND
CADMIUM RED, LIGHT

WHITE WITH A TOUCH OF
THALO GREEN AND RAW SIENNA

BURNT SIENNA, BURNT UMBER
AND CADMIUM RED, LIGHT

When doing quick sketches on the spot, I concentrate on the large foliage areas and pattern created by color and value changes. With my notes of the general range of values and colors, I can rearrange compositions for a more interpretive treatment of the subject in the studio.

A series of exploratory sketches, such as the two on the right, were done very freely with the painting knife using a variety of background colors to determine which was the best over-all middle value background to use for the final painting on page 29. In this manner, I was also able to decide exactly how I wanted to rearrange elements and what kind of over-all statement I wanted to make.

In the first sketch, shown above, I tried a pale ground color of Cadmium Red, Light but found it too intense for the additional play of high intensity color I wanted to use. In the second sketch I used Chromium Oxide Green with a little bit of Burnt Umber. Although the response in this case was more to my liking, I felt that the green detracted from the strong red-orange over-all color statement that I wanted to make. The degree of color intensity in this case was right but the hue was not.

For my final choice, I prepared a canvas in advance by covering it with a rough mixture of Burnt Sienna, Cadmium Red, Light and a slight amount of English Red (Light Red) to keep the first two colors from being too intense. This was allowed to dry thoroughly before the painting was started.

When I decided on the compositional arrangement that best suited me, I sketched it in with a round sable brush using Burnt Umber mixed with Permanent Green, Light and thinned with turpentine. (See Step 1 — page 28.) With a painting knife, I then proceeded to lay in the largest, most dominant over-all color statement of the foliage. For this, I used a mixture of Cadmium Orange and Burnt Sienna. Any of the drawing covered by this lay-in of color was roughly restated. This is only necessary to keep a guide for applying subsequent color areas. Actually, the final painting and manipulation of shapes and areas was done directly with the knife.

In Step 2, you will see the manner in which I continued to build up areas of color. By establishing a middle value to paint on, I was able to work up to lighter areas and back to the darker ones, manipulating these back and forth until I was satisfied with the general effect. Do not concentrate on any one area — work over the entire canvas to bring all sections along at the same time. In this way, you can balance color and make adjustments where necessary. When the general statement is satisfactory, finish up specific areas with the lightest and darkest accents put in last.

This painting uses an analogous color scheme with complementary accent of the most dominant color notes. (The most dominant note, orange, is accented by the blue — and the cool red of the barn acts as a complementary accent to the second most important color statement, the yellow green.) The painting was done almost exclusively with a painting knife.

This method of working relies on the manner in which paint is applied over the rough pre-painted background color for textural effects that suggest rather than completely define rocks, trees, etc. It is important that the composition be planned carefully and later statements made as freely and directly as possible.

Check the tinting strength of each color in small quantities to determine approximate amounts needed in each mixture. In this way, you will avoid mixing more than is needed for a given area. Note that similar colors, with subtle variations, can be arrived at through different mixtures.

ALIZARIN CRIMSON
RAW SIENNA AND WHITE

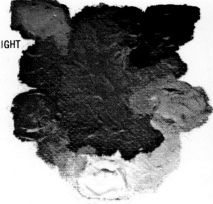

PERMANENT GREEN, LIGHT
BURNT UMBER
RAW SIENNA AND
CADMIUM ORANGE
WITH WHITE

CADMIUM ORANGE
BURNT SIENNA
ENGLISH RED, LIGHT

CADMIUM YELLOW, LIGHT
CADMIUM ORANGE
ENGLISH RED, LIGHT

PERMANENT GREEN, LIGHT
CADMIUM YELLOW, LIGHT
RAW SIENNA

PERMANENT GREEN, LIGHT
RAW SIENNA
CADMIUM ORANGE AND WHITE

For the painting shown in color on pages 32-33, I used the same approach as with the two previous demonstrations. With sketch pad and felt pen, I searched for interesting subjects along the Maine coast. My first sketch, at the top of the page, proved to be a successful composition so it was used for the final painting with the addition of some buildings and boats that I could relate. A later sketch of a lobster boat was used for the large boat element instead of the one in the original sketch. In addition to the sketches, I used the camera for reference on details, etc.

The finished painting was done on a pressed wood panel prepared with four coats of Hyplar Gesso. In preparing such a panel, the Gesso should be allowed to dry between coats and each succeeding coat brushed in a direction opposite the previous one.

When the Gesso was dry, I painted the panel with a mixture of Thalo Blue, French Ultramarine Blue, and Burnt Umber. This was brushed on with a size 16 flat bristle brush. When dry, I used a white pastel stick to sketch in the composition. In addition to linear aspects, I used the pastel to try a spotting of some of the masses, as can be seen in the step on the bottom of page 30.

I painted in all of the larger tonal areas of sky and water first. The buildings and foreground areas followed. The entire panel was developed as quickly as possible. Color and value should be balanced as the work goes along. No one section should be developed too far before getting a spotting of color over-all. I used a combination of painting knives and bristle brushes and in all of the areas let background color come through for richer textural effects. Where an area had too much texture, I reduced it later when the painting was farther along and I could check sections in relation to each other for color, value, and texture. The background color was left untouched for all of the darker masses in the painting.

The colors in the sky were a mixture of Thalo Blue, Burnt Umber, and white in varying degrees. In some spots, the blue is more predominant than in others. I wanted a dramatic effect so the sky was kept quite dark. In the water, I used Thalo Blue and white with touches of Permanent Green, Light and added more French Ultramarine Blue and Burnt Umber to this as I painted foreground areas. As you can see, no attempt was made to put down large flat areas of color. By applying color with the painting knife and varying the spots of color mixed with the Thalo Blue and white, I was able to get a great deal of variety and excitement in this section.

I wanted to maintain a salty, sunbleached, muted effect to the color in the boat, shack, and pilings, etc. so hues were neutralized slightly by mixing complements with white in varying degrees.

Dark accents, deeper than the color of the basic background mixture, were put in with Ivory Black.

I put the painting aside for a few days and then came back for a fresh look and made adjustments that seemed desirable.

The palette used was as follows:

Superba White	Cadmium Red, Light
Thalo Blue	Alizarin Crimson
French Ultramarine Blue	Raw Umber
Permanent Green, Light	Burnt Umber
Cadmium Orange	Ivory Black

THALO BLUE, FRENCH ULTRAMARINE BLUE
AND RAW UMBER

THALO BLUE, BURNT UMBER
AND WHITE

PERMANENT GREEN, LIGHT WITH
RAW UMBER AND WHITE

CADMIUM ORANGE, WHITE AND
A TOUCH OF ALIZARIN CRIMSON

BURNT UMBER AND WHITE WITH A
TOUCH OF PERMANENT GREEN, LIGHT

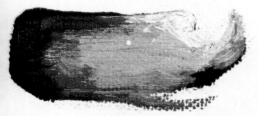

ALIZARIN CRIMSON AND WHITE WITH A
SLIGHT AMOUNT OF THALO BLUE

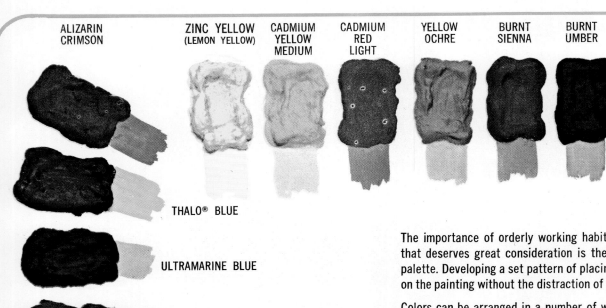

ALIZARIN CRIMSON   ZINC YELLOW (LEMON YELLOW)   CADMIUM YELLOW MEDIUM   CADMIUM RED LIGHT   YELLOW OCHRE   BURNT SIENNA   BURNT UMBER

THALO® BLUE

ULTRAMARINE BLUE

THALO® GREEN

SUPERBA WHITE

The importance of orderly working habits cannot be over emphasized. One that deserves great consideration is the arrangement of the colors on the palette. Developing a set pattern of placing the colors, permits concentration on the painting without the distraction of having to search for a certain color.

Colors can be arranged in a number of ways: — (a) warm along one edge of the palette; cool on another edge — (b) in spectrum sequence — (c) according to color intensity. The important thing is to decide on the one that best suits you. Keep your colors in that order each time you paint.

This is arranged with the warm colors running across the top edge and the cool colors down the side.

BASIC PALETTE

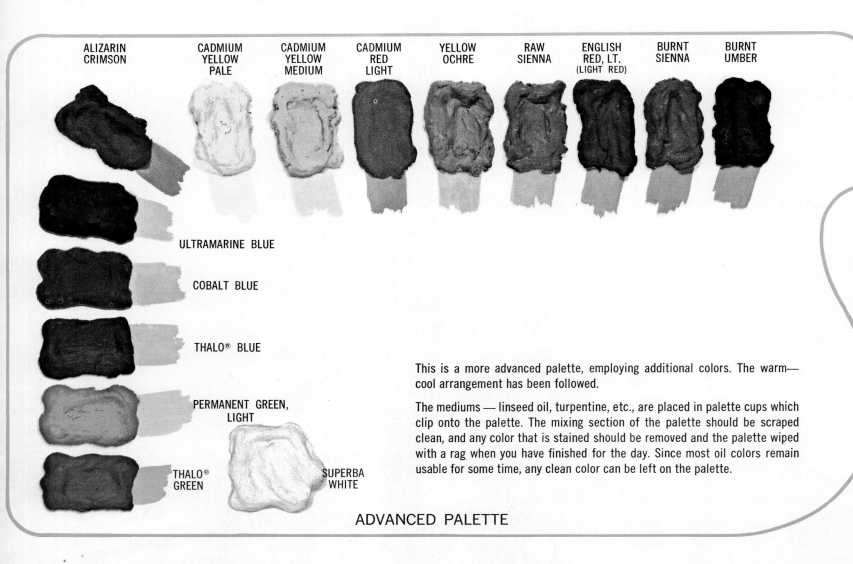

ALIZARIN CRIMSON   CADMIUM YELLOW PALE   CADMIUM YELLOW MEDIUM   CADMIUM RED LIGHT   YELLOW OCHRE   RAW SIENNA   ENGLISH RED, LT. (LIGHT RED)   BURNT SIENNA   BURNT UMBER

ULTRAMARINE BLUE

COBALT BLUE

THALO® BLUE

PERMANENT GREEN, LIGHT

THALO® GREEN   SUPERBA WHITE

This is a more advanced palette, employing additional colors. The warm—cool arrangement has been followed.

The mediums — linseed oil, turpentine, etc., are placed in palette cups which clip onto the palette. The mixing section of the palette should be scraped clean, and any color that is stained should be removed and the palette wiped with a rag when you have finished for the day. Since most oil colors remain usable for some time, any clean color can be left on the palette.

ADVANCED PALETTE

1

2

The impressive range of effects possible with oil color is determined to a large degree by the manner in which the paint is applied. The use of a painting knife for underpainting can leave a surface texture over which, when dry, color can be applied with a knife or brush which hits the high spots of the surface to effect changes in color. Scumbling, the application of additional color with a fairly dry brush, can give you softer textures and changes in color. Glazing with thin washes of color provides even more subtle color changes.

These photographs show some techniques which may be used:

The rag can be used for a soft blending of colors in certain areas. (See #1 above) Rags should be soft and absorbent—old shirts or worn sheets are quite good.

The painting knife is shown in #2 being used to scrape color from the painting to allow the texture of the canvas to show through for greater variety and interest in the area.

The bristle brush (#3) is shown being used to scumble fairly dry color over a previously painted section of the canvas which had dried.

In #4 a smaller painting knife is being used for the delicate application of color over an impasto section of the underpainting. The dark underpainting shows through for a variety of fascinating textures.

3

4

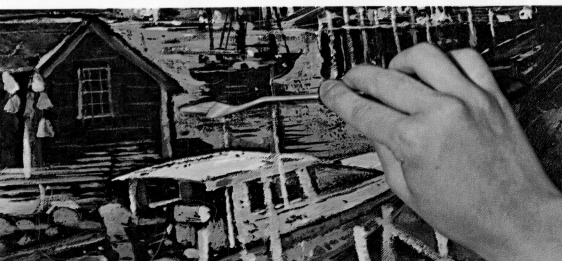

This demonstration was prepared by Dean Ellis, a well known painter whose work appears in many public and private collections.

This abstract of surf and rocks was executed in oil on a pressed wood panel which had been prepared with Hyplar Gesso. As a preliminary to painting, the panel was covered with a ground color consisting of Burnt Umber, Thalo Crimson, and Mars Black. For this ground color, I used Hyplar polymer colors which make an excellent underpainting for oils and dry very rapidly. The color was brushed over the panel very loosely without regard to the ultimate design of the painting.

In Step 1, the basic masses were sketched in with a light pastel in the broadest possible terms. Next, the surface was sprayed with Retouch Varnish and the painting started. The purpose of the varnish was to 'fix' the pastel and to provide a slightly tacky surface into which I could work with oils. The sky, about a middle value equal to that of the background color, was laid in with a painting knife and rags, allowing the underpainting to show through in spots.

Next, in Step 2, the darker values were developed, and at the same time lighter color values introduced. The purpose was to move the painting as rapidly as possible to its

ALIZARIN CRIMSON AND BURNT UMBER WITH A SPOT OF IVORY BLACK

COBALT BLUE AND WHITE MODIFIED WITH IVORY BLACK

ultimate color and value range. The smaller, more detailed forms and subtle colors were developed in keeping with the desired feeling and mood. Painting knives were used to establish the linear pattern of the painting after the colors had reached a suitable degree of tackiness.

ULTRAMARINE RED, YELLOW OCHRE
AND A TOUCH OF BURNT UMBER

BURNT UMBER, THALO GREEN
AND YELLOW OCHRE

ULTRAMARINE RED, WHITE AND A
TOUCH OF ALIZARIN CRIMSON

ULTRAMARINE RED, COBALT BLUE AND
WHITE WITH A SPOT OF IVORY BLACK

Colors in the rock mass, derived from notes and recollections of rocks and algae along the shore, were held to darker values to imply solidity. As a final step, edges were given considerable attention, sharpening them in certain instances for maximum contrast and softening them in others for variety.

The oil color palette for this painting was as follows:

Superba White	Cobalt Blue
Cadmium Orange	French Ultramarine Blue
Yellow Ochre	Thalo Green
Alizarin Crimson	Ultramarine Red
Burnt Umber	Ivory Black

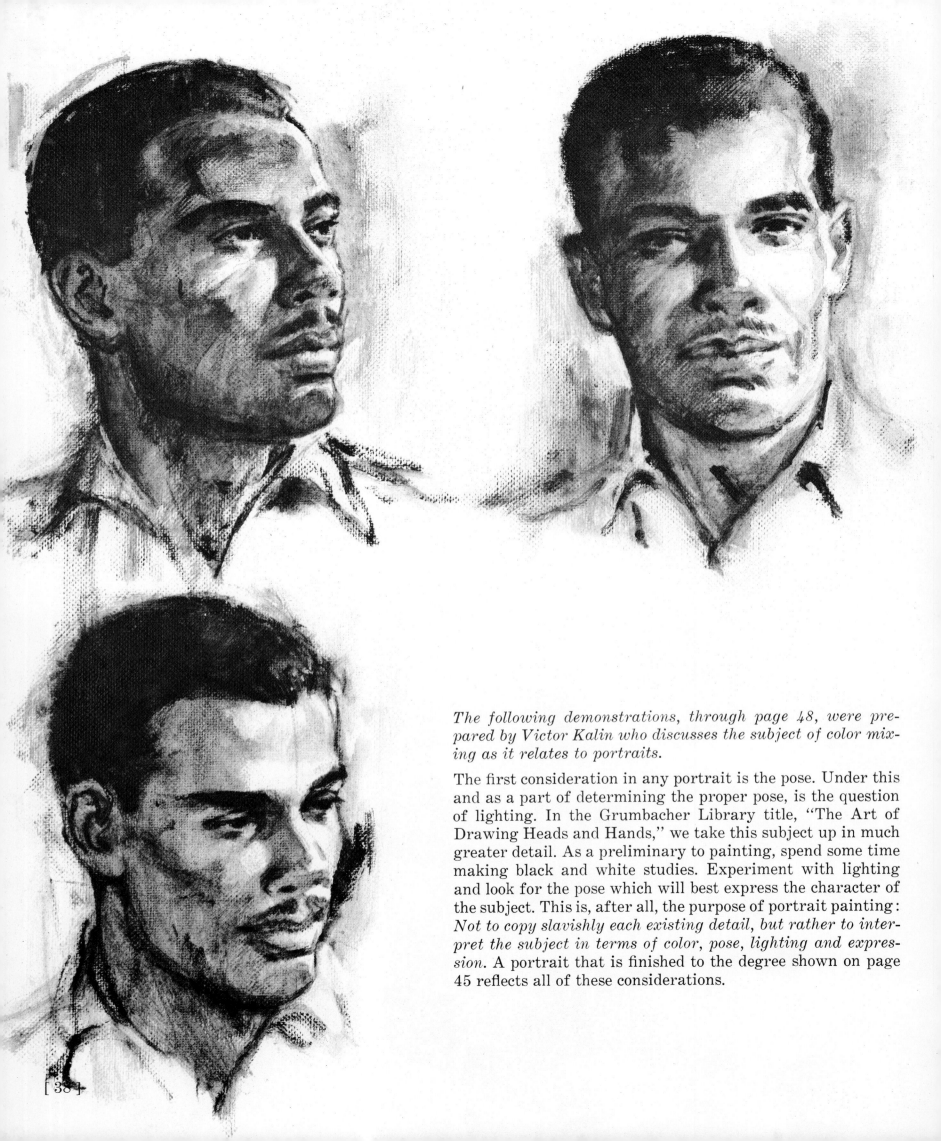

The following demonstrations, through page 48, were prepared by Victor Kalin who discusses the subject of color mixing as it relates to portraits.

The first consideration in any portrait is the pose. Under this and as a part of determining the proper pose, is the question of lighting. In the Grumbacher Library title, "The Art of Drawing Heads and Hands," we take this subject up in much greater detail. As a preliminary to painting, spend some time making black and white studies. Experiment with lighting and look for the pose which will best express the character of the subject. This is, after all, the purpose of portrait painting: *Not to copy slavishly each existing detail, but rather to interpret the subject in terms of color, pose, lighting and expression.* A portrait that is finished to the degree shown on page 45 reflects all of these considerations.

When making these preliminary studies, work in whatever medium is most comfortable for you. Pencil, charcoal, or use the brush with a single color. By careful observation and analysis, you will find characteristics which best express the subject with forthright definition.

As an example, note the softer, less angular quality of form in women and children as compared to the angular, well defined planes in a man's head. Concentration on hair, eyes, and lips and subtle handling of form in the rest of the head will help to express a woman's characteristics better than labored definition of the structure of the head.

The drawings on these pages are the preliminary studies for paintings shown on pages 41 and 45.

[39]

In this portrait, an analogous color scheme is used. The colors are within a very close range and values run a fairly complete range from dark to light.

1. The head was sketched in with a mixture of Raw Sienna and Burnt Sienna thinned with turpentine and the shadow areas put in with a heavier mixture of this same combination. The background was partially blocked in with a mixture of Yellow Ochre, Cadmium Yellow, Light, a touch of Thalo Green, and white. The shirt is a mixture of Alizarin Crimson and Cadmium Orange. The drawing was restated with a darker mixture of Burnt Sienna and Ultramarine Blue.

2. In this step, the complete blocking in of all the color areas prior to finishing up any one section can be seen.

The portrait was finished by refining areas, picking up accents, softening and blending edges where necessary and adding texture to the background by applying additional color with the painting knife.

BURNT SIENNA
YELLOW OCHRE
FRENCH ULTRAMARINE BLUE
WITH WHITE

YELLOW OCHRE
THALO GREEN
BURNT SIENNA

CADMIUM ORANGE
ALIZARIN CRIMSON

YELLOW OCHRE
CADMIUM YELLOW, PALE
THALO GREEN WITH WHITE

RAW SIENNA
BURNT SIENNA

FRENCH ULTRAMARINE BLUE
BURNT SIENNA

Children are probably the most difficult of models because their attention span is so short. They become bored with the business and tend to show this in their expressions. This is not necessarily bad and can quite frequently result in a more appealing portrait. Spend the time mixing colors while they are resting between poses.

A complementary color scheme was used for the portrait on page 44. The progressive steps in the development of the painting from a linear rendition to the massing of color are shown on the facing page.

The drawing in Step 1 was sketched in on the canvas with Yellow Ochre thinned with turpentine and as quickly as possible the white of the canvas was covered. For the background Thalo Green with a little Yellow Ochre was used and in the dark areas, some Burnt Sienna was added to this mixture. The shirt was a mixture of Cadmium Red, Light; Alizarin Crimson and Cadmium Yellow, Pale. The shadow areas of the face and hands were blocked in with Burnt Sienna; Cadmium Red, Light; Yellow Ochre and a touch of Thalo Green. After this the lighter flesh areas were put in using White mixed with very small quantities of Yellow Ochre; Cadmium Red, Light; Alizarin Crimson, and to cool this mixture slightly, a touch of Thalo Green.

In painting, you should carefully examine and indicate the shapes of the shadow areas. Generally, in portraiture, the shadows are painted cool to effect a contrast with the normally warm, lighter flesh tones. However, this relationship can be reversed. It is best to exclude white from dark shadow color mixtures. The amount of color needed in each mixture is best determined by mixing very small quantities in advance. For the lighter tints, start with white and add color slowly. For the darker, more chromatic colors, start with the most predominant color in the mixture and modify this carefully.

The painting was finished by blending areas between the light and dark, painting intermediate values in the light areas, and picking up accents wherever needed.

The palette used for this painting was: Superba White; Yellow Ochre; Cadmium Yellow, Pale; Cadimum Red, Light; Alizarin Crimson; Burnt Sienna; Burnt Umber; French Ultramarine Blue; and Thalo Green.

In the Portrait on page 45, the same palette was used. The model's opalescent skin tones are balanced by the stronger colors of her clothing. Basically, the shadows of the skin are cool, tending toward a soft violet gray. The addition of various reflected colors helps with the modeling and provides both interest and variety in the flesh areas.

Colors used on the background and clothing are shown next to the painting. The light flesh color was a mixture of white with very small quantities of Yellow Ochre; Cadmium Red, Light; Alizarin Crimson and to cool this slightly, Thalo Green was used. The soft violet grays in the shadow area are the result of mixing small quantities of Yellow Ochre; Alizarin Crimson; Burnt Sienna; and French Ultramarine Blue with white. Experiment with your mixtures for painting warm and cool shadow colors. The slight reduction in the intensity of a flesh color might be sufficient to indicate the turning of a plane.

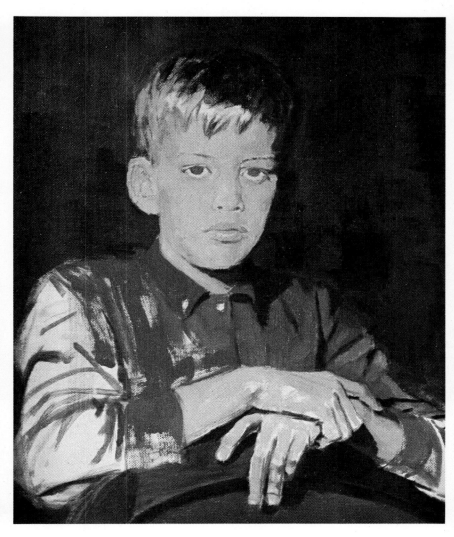

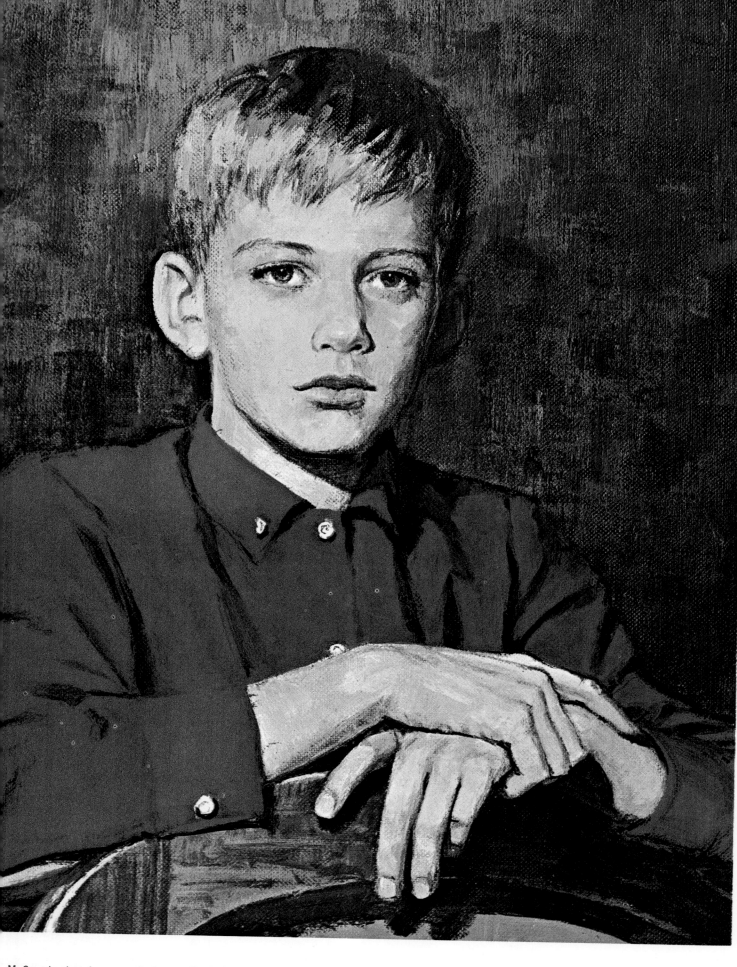

YELLOW OCHRE
BURNT SIENNA
THALO GREEN

THALO GREEN
YELLOW OCHRE
CADMIUM RED, LIGHT
ALIZARIN CRIMSON
WITH WHITE

BURNT SIENNA
ALIZARIN CRIMSON
THALO GREEN

ALIZARIN CRIMSON
BURNT UMBER

M. Grumbacher, Inc. manufactures a Flesh Color to simplify mixing when painting portraits. This color can be modified with additional color for a great variety of subtle skin tones. At the right, we show some of the many modifications possible.

FLESH

CHROMIUM OXIDE GREEN ADDED

FRENCH ULTRAMARINE BLUE
YELLOW OCHRE
THALO GREEN
WITH WHITE

CADMIUM RED, LIGHT
YELLOW OCHRE
THALO GREEN
ALIZARIN CRIMSON
WITH WHITE

YELLOW OCHRE
FRENCH ULTRAMARINE BLUE
ALIZARIN CRIMSON
BURNT SIENNA
WITH WHITE

CADMIUM YELLOW, PALE
CADMIUM RED, LIGHT
ALIZARIN CRIMSON
BURNT UMBER

YELLOW OCHRE ADDED

GRUMBACHER RED ADDED

MARS VIOLET ADDED

46]

Photographs can be used to capture a pose when dealing with a restless subject. These should, however, be suplemented with your own careful observation and drawings. As can be seen in these pastel studies, the light and shadow areas have been kept as simple as possible, almost flat, and they still retain all the feeling of form necessary. Pastel is an ideal medium for quick color notes as well as more finished paintings.

An unusual method of handling a standard subject is by the use of back lighting. This throws the subject into shadow and the initial effect is a silhouetted shape against the background. This creates a challenging and interesting problem because the modeling of form must be accomplished by the most subtle changes in both color and value.

The basic flesh tones in the painting on page 48 are represented by the two upper mixtures. The uppermost, by introducing Alizarin Crimson, is cooler than the second employing Burnt Sienna. As flesh tones, they require little modification to achieve the range of values found in the face. The third mixture is basic for the darks. The fourth is for general light areas.

In an analysis of this painting, it can be seen that areas sparkle as the result of color similar in value and intensity but varying greatly in hue. The background is alive with tints of yellow, pink, green, blue, and brown, yet the over-all effect is of a single graded tone when seen from a distance. The same juxaposition of color is present throughout the painting. By maintaining a close value range within each area, it is possible to use a variety of color and still maintain a feeling of unity.

Start by blocking in general color areas as shown in the previous demonstrations and gradually build up texture with scumbling and glazing, adjusting areas to each other as you go along. Sections that seem too strong can be scraped or left to dry and then reworked to bring them back into balance.

The palette used for this painting was as follows:

Superba White	
Cadmium Yellow, Pale	Burnt Sienna
Cadmium Red, Light	Burnt Umber
Alizarin Crimson	Thalo Green
French Ultramarine Blue	Yellow Ochre

YELLOW OCHRE
CADMIUM RED, LIGHT
ALIZARIN CRIMSON
THALO GREEN
CADMIUM YELLOW, PALE

CADMIUM RED, LIGHT
YELLOW OCHRE
BURNT SIENNA
THALO GREEN
CADMIUM YELLOW, PALE

THALO GREEN
YELLOW OCHRE
ALIZARIN CRIMSON
BURNT UMBER

SUPERBA WHITE WITH
THALO GREEN
YELLOW OCHRE
FRENCH ULTRAMARINE BLUE
ALIZARIN CRIMSON

OIL PAINTING DEMONSTRATIONS

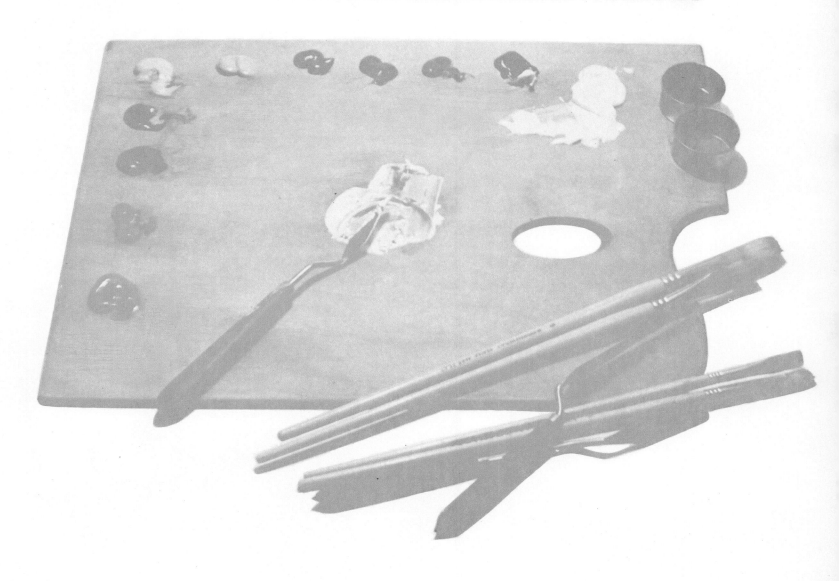

1

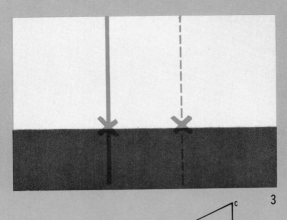

2

3

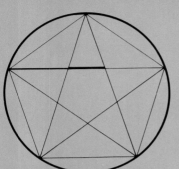

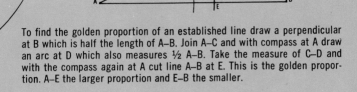

The Greeks developed a mathematical formula to define what they considered the most pleasing division of a line or space. It was called the "Golden Proportion" and during the Italian renaissance "The Divine Proportion." Based on the Pentagram, in terms of measurement it is a division in which the smaller part is in the same proportion to the greater part as the greater part is to the whole.

To find the length of a line to form a golden proportion with line A–B. Drop a perpendicular line the same length as A–B. With the compass point at ½ A–B and extended to C draw an arc which cuts the line at D. A–B is then the larger measure of a golden proportion with B–D the smaller proportion.

To find the golden proportion of an established line draw a perpendicular at B which is half the length of A–B. Join A–C and with compass at A draw an arc at D which also measures ½ A–B. Take the measure of C–D and with the compass again at A cut line A–B at E. This is the golden proportion. A–E the larger proportion and E–B the smaller.

4

5

6

7

For the student about to start the first painting, the blank canvas can be somewhat intimidating. How to place the subject on the canvas, how big to make it, where to place the center of interest, are all considerations which must be determined before the painting can start.

The following points on composition are not an attempt to set up formulas or rules, (rules can be broken without jeopardizing the success of a painting), rather these are a framework by which the student may more quickly arrive at conclusions of his own based on the kind of statement he wants to make about the subject involved.

Size and proportion are, of course, determined to a great degree by the subject. Bizarre or unusual proportions have a tendency to take on a distracting importance.

Compositions may be built upon triangles, circles, squares, or any other geometric or non-geometric form but must maintain a balance between dominant and subordinate elements within the overall defined area of the canvas. Whether realistic or abstract, each part of the painting must work well with relation to all other parts.

In order to maintain compositional unity, equal distribution of space, as in figure 1, should be avoided so that areas do not compete with each other for attention. In figures 2 and 3 we show dominant and subordinate areas which work together vertically and horizontally. The X's indicate points at which the center of interest might be placed. There should, of course, be just one center of interest. Two equally important statements within a painting will compete with each other and the painting will suffer as a result. There can and should be other statements in a painting but each should be an interesting counterpoint to the major center of interest.

Traps to be avoided are the diagonal split, (figure 4) which creates competing areas of equal or almost equal size, and awkward tangents or alignment of shapes (figure 5) which call too much attention to themselves.

In figure 6 we see that a strong horizontal statement, while suggesting a peaceful feeling, can be monotonous. Diagonal (figure 7), or circular lines suggest movement and action while vertical lines imply dignity.

Contrast of values, the intensity of color, pattern, or shape—any of these can be used to create the focal point of the painting.

In a painting negative background areas and positive subject areas are equally important (C). For example: Any awkward shapes occurring in the background area between a tree and house in a landscape painting will cause a distracting quality in the overall painting.

A and B indicate the lines of direction in these paintings which direct the eye to the center of interest. Time spent analyzing paintings broadens the understanding of the variety and personal interpretation that each artist applies to composition.

A

B

C

ZING OR "SUPERBA" WHITE

CADMIUM YELLOW, LIGHT

YELLOW OCHRE

BURNT SIENNA

COBALT BLUE

FRENCH ULTRAMARINE BLUE

THALO GREEN

CADMIUM RED, LIGHT

ALIZARIN CRIMSON

STILL LIFE

Victor Kalin demonstrates the versatility of a limited palette with still life and some very delicate flower subjects.

Here is a simple plan in approaching color mixing. Use the palette knife to mix each color with increasing amounts of white, to discover how colors change. By mixing each color from full strength to the palest tints, you will become aware of the hundreds of gradations available. This test will determine the potential of each new color as you add it to your palette.

Wait until you have completed several paintings with the palette shown before adding additional colors; then add a color at a time, selecting one that will be of particular help with a specific subject. Mix each color with each of the remaining colors. The tones created by mixing two colors can then be mixed with white to add an almost unlimited range of new colors. Consider the additional variations that

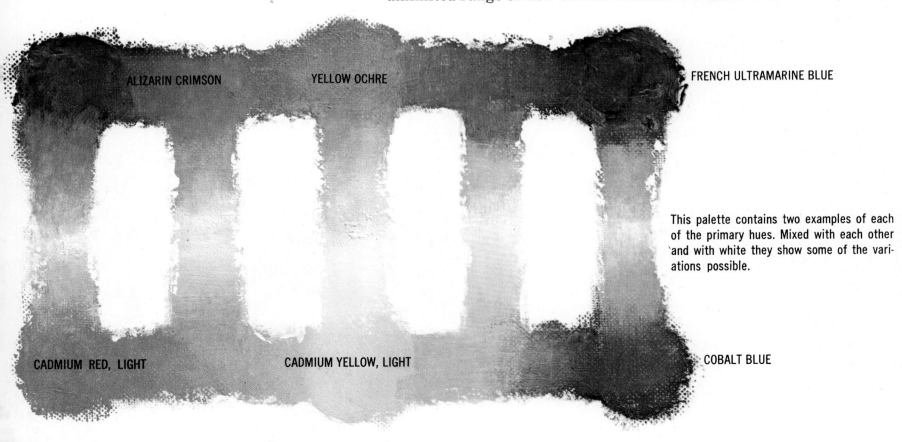

ALIZARIN CRIMSON   YELLOW OCHRE   FRENCH ULTRAMARINE BLUE

This palette contains two examples of each of the primary hues. Mixed with each other and with white they show some of the variations possible.

CADMIUM RED, LIGHT   CADMIUM YELLOW, LIGHT   COBALT BLUE

52]

three or more colors will make when mixed together and lightened with white. You will find that the fewer colors you use to achieve a certain result, the less likelihood there will be that the mixture will look "muddy."

A very serviceable black which produces the most beautiful pearly grays as white is added, can be made by mixing Alizarin Crimson and Thalo Green.

For a painting medium start with a mixture of one-quarter linseed oil and three quarters turpentine, gradually increasing the oil to one-half as the painting progresses. This helps to prevent a dulling of the color which sometimes occurs as the paint dries. A spray of retouch varnish will bring back the gloss and freshness of color when this does occur.

When you are through painting for the day, scrape the mixed colors off your palette and wipe it clean with turpentine and a rag. Leave the squeezed out pure colors around the edge; they will remain useable for several days. Give each a drop of linseed oil to keep it fresh, and wipe the palette with a bit of oil. Clean your brushes with turpentine and wash them thoroughly with soap and water. Be sure to get all the paint out of the bristles near the metal ferrule.

This sketch of fruit was painted with a palette limited to three primary colors, Alizarin Crimson, Cadmium Yellow, Light, and French Ultramarine Blue plus white. A warm red (Cadmium Red, Light) would have produced more accurate color tones for the apples and the orange, but would have made it impossible to mix a clean purple for the plums and the grapes. A simple exercise such as this will show you the desirability of both a warm red (Cadmium Red, Light) and a cold red—(Alizarin Crimson) for your palette.

(1)

(2)

In this series of photographs we have tried to show that a single set-up can produce any number of interesting pictures depending on the point of view. Nothing in the arrangement was touched and yet by moving from one location to another, complete changes in both composition and mood were achieved. By means of a second color overlay you can see the flat geometric shape suggested by each viewpoint. These shapes, together with the linear movements found in both the flow of drapery and the lines of the subjects themselves, help to establish the design of each picture. Notice how the strong vertical pattern of light and shadow in the drapery produces a feeling for a taller-than-wide picture despite the fact that the bowl of fruit itself suggests a basically horizontal composition. These principles can be applied to any arrangement of objects. You will find that balance of mass and line is easier to achieve by arranging your still life studies to produce naturally pleasing effects than by consciously attempting to make your objects fit into a rigid geometric pattern. As the elements are grouped look at them from several different directions in order not to overlook the best angle.

(3)

It is best to limit your set-up to simple objects and a bit of drapery for your first painting. Don't try to paint anything too delicate or dainty; instead, pick things with simple bold lines and textures, such as crockery, brass, or copper.

Arrange your objects where they will not be disturbed for the several days you will be working with them. The most consistent light throughout the day is from a north window. Any light source, whether natural or artificial, should be consistent.

Combine shapes that will contrast with each other in size, color, and texture—metal with ceramic, dull with shiny, tall with short, etc. Avoid fresh fruit and flowers for your first experiments. Such material seldom looks the same the next day and after several days become virtually unuseable.

In a simple still life, or even a complicated one, the drape often plays an important role. Not only does it add color but the swing of the folds in the material can contribute to the strength of the composition. Hang a piece of cloth on the wall and see how much more interesting your objects become when complemented by the color, texture, and design which the drape provides.

After you have arranged the set-up to your satisfaction and picked the best angle from which to view it, determine the shape of the picture. Now sketch the subject on your canvas. Simply block in the bold shapes and indicate the folds of the drapery. With this rough indication of the light and shadow areas, you have started painting.

Pick a large area of color, possibly the drapery, and duplicate it with paint. Mix this color on your palette using a knife, and when you have found it, brush some on the canvas. This color, both on the canvas and the palette, can be a guide for your next color. Is it lighter or darker? Warmer or colder? Brighter or grayer? As you mix each color check it against the others. It is easier to compare proper color values against each other than against the white of the bare canvas. If a color is wrong, don't hesitate to scrape it off the canvas with your knife and try again. It will look just as fresh as the previous one. This is one quality which makes oil paint such an excellent medium for the beginning painter.

(4)

(5)

(6)

1

This combination of lemons, limes, brass bowl, and drape was picked as an exercise to demonstrate the range of variation in light and shadow of the color yellow. This exercise will help you understand how the color deepens in value and is affected by surrounding colors. Beginners sometimes have a great deal of difficulty with this problem.

1. The subject is sketched in using turpentine and a tint of Yellow Ochre. The overall shape, the folds of the drapery, and a rough indication of the light and shadow areas are all that is necessary at this stage.

2. The masses of the drapery, the fruit, and the dark areas are spotted in over the entire canvas. No attempt is made at this stage to develop any one section.

2

3

4

5

Thalo Green with Cadmium Yellow, Light is used for the green of the limes. For some of the warmer yellows, a touch of Cadmium Red, Light is mixed with the Cadmium Yellow, Light.

3. As the canvas is developed further, the Yellow Ochre of the drapery is given interest and variety by mixing slight amounts of other colors with it. A touch of Thalo Green makes the Yellow Ochre cooler, and a spot of Alizarin Crimson makes it warmer. The overall background color is basically a mixture of Yellow Ochre and French Ultramarine Blue with white.

4. The canvas by now is almost completely covered except for the highlight areas

of the brass bowl. The darks, a mixture of Alizarin Crimson, Thalo Green, Burnt Sienna, and French Ultramarine Blue with white used sparingly, give accent and form to the fruit and bowl.

5. At this stage, color and the dark accents that define shape and form can be worked back and forth until the statements gradually become what you want them to be.

Some edges softened, others made crisp and bold, all contribute to the interest and quality of your finished canvas and make your still life painting something more than a slavish copy of nature. The final touches should be the highlights on the bowl and fruit.

157

As shown opposite, a painting knife makes a crisp petal for a zinnia, or a daisy, while your thumb might be just the thing to blend the subtle shading found in the recesses of a rose.

FLOWERS

The techniques of flower painting range from abstract blobs of pure color (from the tube) to the most minutely detailed renderings of bouquets, complete with dew drops and insects.

Remember that flowers, even the hardiest, last only a few days. If you are a week end painter you must either paint quickly or try to remember what the bouquet looked like a week earlier when it was fresher. The new plastic flowers make excellent models and offer a solution to this problem.

Examine each individual flower or cluster of blossoms and try to establish its basic shape. Is it, for example, a cone, ball, or cup? Each flower is a three-dimensional object and has a light side and a dark side, casts a shadow, and is affected by the light reflected from the colors of its environment. Look for its structure. Does it consist of many small blossoms or is it a single bloom? Is it concave or convex? Are the petals in single or multiple rows, ragged or smooth edged? With your paint try to recreate this character—first, by defining it in its boldest terms of light and shadow, later by adding the details.

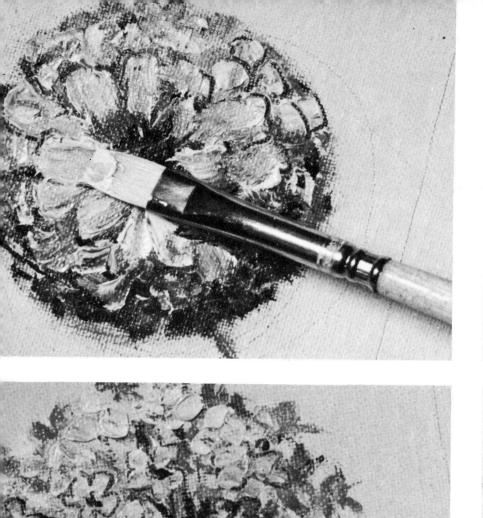

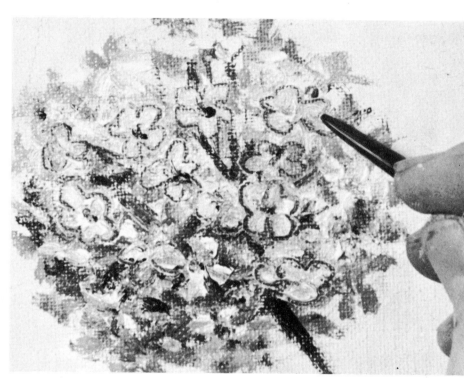

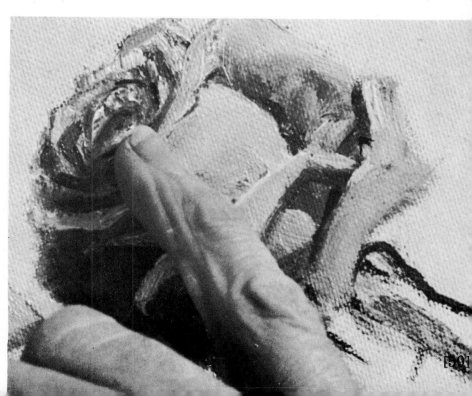

1

This study of bachelor buttons and wild daisies illustrates some possibilities in a grouping of flowers. Unlike our clinical consideration on the previous page, here each flower becomes a part of the whole painting and in some cases nothing more than an indication of overall form or a spot of color.

2

1. The rough composition is blocked in using a mixture of Cobalt Blue with white; Yellow Ochre is used in spots for the drawing. This establishes the pattern on the canvas.

2. The entire canvas is worked over at this stage to cover it with color. The background is basically Cobalt Blue grayed slightly with Burnt Sienna, in spots mixed with Yellow Ochre and white. The spotting of the yellow daisy centers balances with the pink of the bachelor buttons against the blue background.

3. As the painting progresses, some of the flowers are painted out; others added. Dark accents, a mixture of Thalo Green with a touch of Alizarin Crimson, are added and adjustments made to balance table top and background color as well as the pattern of flowers. Treating the picture as a whole rather than as a series of separate parts is the secret of producing a painting that "hangs together". The stripes of the vase added at this stage appear overpowering and so are painted out, to be added later when the flowers are further developed.

3

4. The flowers are brought to a completed stage. Note that most of the daisy petals are not pure white they are grayed to keep a proper relationship with the painting as a whole. The foreground petals are the only ones brought up close to pure white. These and other highlights are put in last. The darker accents of the leaves and stalks help to concentrate interest on the flowers themselves.

To add interest to large areas such as the background, experiment with the variety that is possible by graying the Cobalt Blue with Burnt Sienna and warming if slightly with Yellow Ochre or cooling it with Thalo Green.

4

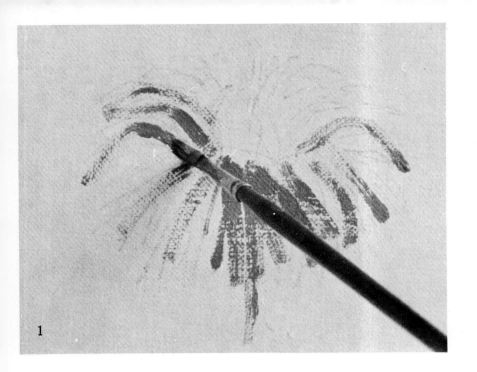

These illustrations show the painting development of two distinct types of blossoms: the Aster and the Lilac. These basic steps of blocking in the general shape, indicating shadow area for a feeling of form, and creating the higher values and accents can be used for painting any flower.

With the Aster, Step 1 was to block in the form by painting the petals from the center outward, employing a middle value of the color of the flower. In Step 2, darker values were painted in, still following the form, and in Step 3, lighter values start to give the blossom a feeling of volume. The final step was to blend colors where necessary and add accents of color to the completed painting for sparkle.

3

4

Step 1 in the Lilac, consists of painting the over-all shape of the blossom in a middle value of the color of the flower. The deeper values in Step 2 are put in next to indicate the shadow areas. In Step 3, the transition between the middle and dark values is blended with an intermediate color. As a final step, the higher values are painted following the shape of individual blossoms. These blossoms, although they are all quite light, should not be painted with the identical color. Some subtle variation in the higher values will avoid monotony and give the final painting a greater feeling of dimension.

1

2

Here is an example of flower painting by Mr. Kalin that explores a somewhat different approach. The charm of this painting lies more in the surface texture of the paint, the excitement of the colors, and the strong dark shape of the silhouette than in a realistic representation.

1. The subject is roughly blocked in, using Yellow Ochre diluted with turpentine. No attempt at detail is necessary at this stage. Detail will come with the development of the painting.

2. The background is added in an inpasto manner, using a fast drying underpainting white (MG® White). Yellow Ochre, Cadmium Yellow, Light; and Cadmium Red, Light are brushed on the canvas in spots as the white is brushed on. Thalo

3

4

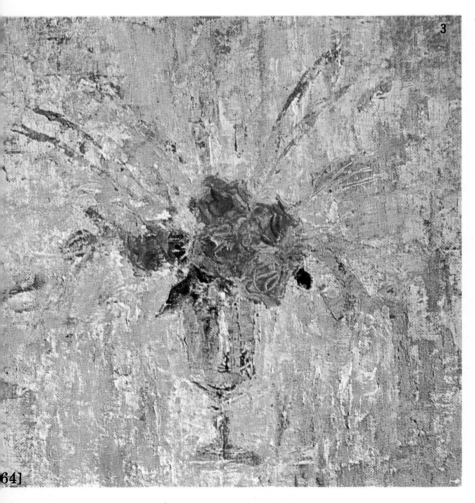

Green, used on the leaf forms, is also introduced lightly into the background. Throughout the development of this painting, as colors are introduced to the subject, they are first brushed on lightly and later, with the palette knife, put in more heavily into the background.

3. At this point the painting knife replaces brushes. The roses are developed using Cadmium Red, Light and white. Cadmium Red, Light mixed with Alizarin Crimson is used for accents. The leaf forms are indicated using Thalo Green mixed with Alizarin Crimson accented in spots with Cobalt Blue. The background texture is the result of painting, scraping, glazing, and reworking color over color until the desired value and surface texture are reached.

4. Now the painting is almost completed. All that remains is the placing of accents, insertion of details, indication of color notes on the crystal, and a general working over the entire canvas for final adjustments that make for the maximum unity.

In the final painting we see the adjustments made from step four. The basic silhouette still holds, but the relationship to background is much more subtle in spots, while the additional colors glazed over the background add even more interest. Spots of Thalo Green; Cadmium Yellow, Light; Yellow Ochre; Alizarin Crimson; and Cadmium Red, Light, all mixed individually with white and put in with the painting knife, give a final sparkle to the background.

WILLOW

APPLE

PINE

MAPLE

LAUREL

ELM

CEDAR

LANDSCAPE

Christopher Davis, a versatile painter with a variety of approaches for achieving richly textured surfaces in landscapes and seascapes, discusses approaching the landscape — through page 73.

An important element of the landscape is the tree, either by itself or as part of the overall composition. *The importance of the basic silhouette, whether in drawing or painting, cannot be over emphasized.* If it is correct, your statement of the tree is well on its way. It is a simple matter to indicate depth of form by the addition of light areas and additional dark accents. Practice drawing or painting the simple contour shapes.

When painting, mass in the general over all shape with a brush and work your pattern of dark and light with a palette or painting knife for a textural quality appropriate to that of most foliage. As your facility increases, study the great variety of textures in different species and develop your personal approach to the indication of such textures as directly as possible without getting fussy or labored in the painting.

While it is not necessary to draw the skeleton of the tree in each case, you should have a feeling for, and understanding of, the structure and growth. This is necessary for proper placing of branches in the mass of foliage as well as indicating the basic silhouette to begin with.

Depth is created by the interplay of light and shadow.

Add variety by studying the patterns created by light against dark.

Study the pattern created by the direction of light. Mass the foliage by means of color of middle value; then add darks and lights.

Keep distant bushes massed and simple.

Note the spread at the base; trees do not go into the ground like sticks.

Foreground branches and foliage are dark; distance is suggested by lighter background areas.

[67

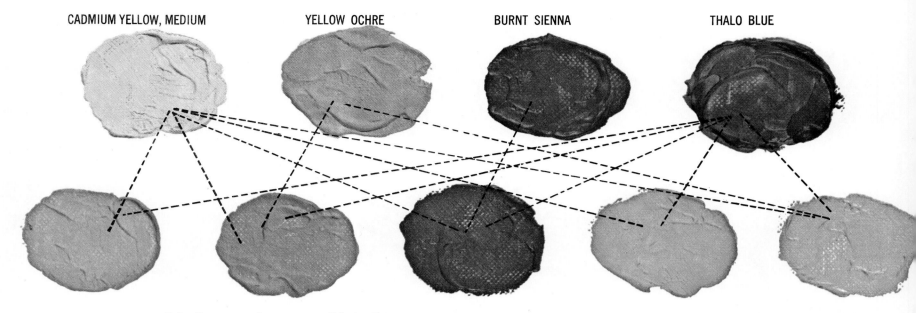

CADMIUM YELLOW, MEDIUM   YELLOW OCHRE   BURNT SIENNA   THALO BLUE

Note the range of greens possible by the addition of white and intermixtures of the colors shown.

As an example of what can be obtained from a limited palette, the sketches on this page and the page opposite were painted with the colors shown next to them. While it is true that some subjects lend themselves to a limited palette more readily than others, it is better to learn to work within a limitation and increase the palette as you come to understand the complete range possible with each inter-mixture. Much more control over a full palette of colors can be gained in this way.

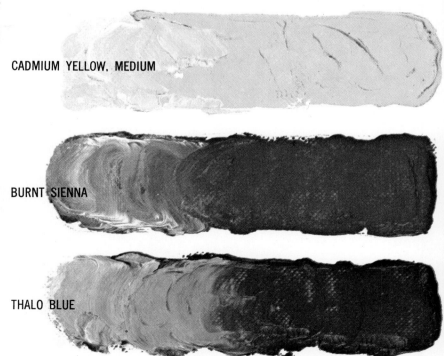

CADMIUM YELLOW, MEDIUM

BURNT SIENNA

THALO BLUE

CADMIUM ORANGE

THALO BLUE

FRENCH ULTRAMARINE BLUE

BURNT SIENNA

CADMIUM YELLOW, LIGHT

ALIZARIN CRIMSON

THALO BLUE

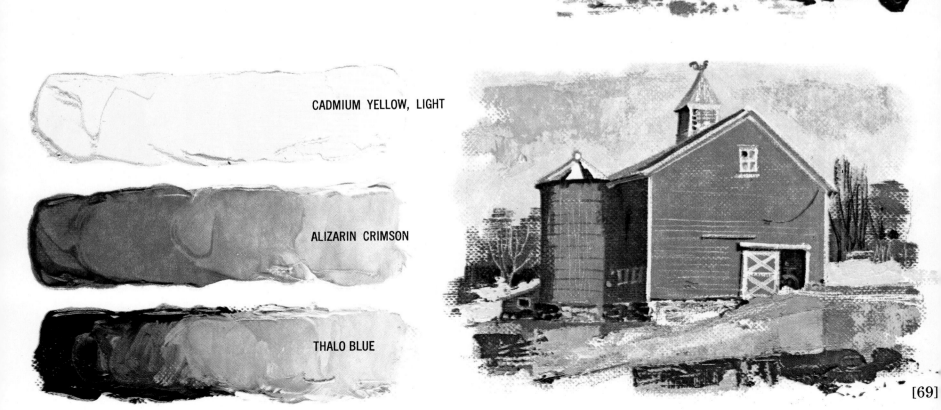

Felt tip pen

Outdoor studies can be quick sketches like some of the examples shown here, or more detailed drawings, like those on the following pages.

Try various media — felt pen, brush and ink, or water color lamp black, in addition to the charcoal, carbon or lead pencil. Find the one that suits your particular need and interest. Sumi Black Paste Ink (Rend Ink) with brush can give you quick tonal studies and wonderful textures.

With quick sketches it is sometimes a good idea to write in various color notes as reminders for painting later. You will be surprised how helpful they can be in recalling the overall mood and color scheme.

Felt tip pen

Felt tip pen

[70]

Lamp black wash.

Wash is ideal for quick notes. The side of the brush used wet or dry (as with the shingle siding and rocks) can give you a wonderful range of textures.

With this sketch the pattern was the important thing, although there is enough detail and indication of form to use for a more finished painting.

Rend Ink

[71]

Clouds that shift suddenly can be indicated directly and quickly with a palette or painting knife. Watch the overall shapes. Study the variety of types—edges hard, soft, wispy, stormy.

In approaching the landscape don't worry about minor details at the beginning. They can be filled in later if the painting seems to demand it. After the composition has been sketched in, look for the overall effect and paint it as directly as possible with brush or knife.

After sketching out your composition and completing basic lay-ins of color, try different ways of indicating the textures of various subjects. Half close your eyes and look for the broadest pattern of dark and light.

Mass distant trees; indicate form of trunks simply, either with knife, by scraping out, or with small brush.

The texture and color in a rock mass can be very exciting. Capturing the effect in paint is an interesting challenge. Work out the pattern of the darks; then with the knife or brush, work into this dark mass with slightly lighter browns, blues, etc. Now apply your colors of lighter value and work the desired texture into the wet paint.

For a delicate warm gray, mix Yellow Ochre, Cobalt Violet, and white. The shadow in the cloud should be on the warm side. Look for the great color variety to be found in clouds. In this case the finger was used to blend edges quickly.

The painting knife is an excellent tool not only for laying in color, but also for drawing into wet color to indicate textures, as with this old tree trunk, and for simple indication of tall grass. The knife also keeps one from getting too fussy with detail in the early stages.

For sketching, a pen or charcoal with a suggestion of
ink wash gives a sufficient range for values and textures

Many painters limit their time on location to making studies in black and white. In the studio they re-arrange the elements of this material in a highly creative consideration of the subject. In the following landscape demonstrations (through page 89) Albert John Pucci shows his approach and discusses his technique of painting.

As the illustrations show, I make one major drawing and additional detailed drawings of the areas that in-

terest me most. Various compositional possibilities are worked out in black and white and my notes supplemented with photographs.

I find I can be more creative away from location, taking more liberties to strengthen the composition by moving trees, buildings, paths, etc. By spending my time in the field gathering information in this manner, I often have material for many paintings rather than simply the one I might have had if I tried painting on the spot.

1

After the composition had been resolved and the drawing worked up to the size of the canvas, I proceeded in the following manner:

1. The entire canvas was covered with the colors of a middle value that were most dominant in the subject, using a brush or palette knife. In this instance I used a mixture of Raw Umber, Lemon Yellow, Thalo Green, Green Earth and white to arrive at the color I wanted. Color was squeezed out in enough quantity for the size of the canvas and mixed directly on the surface. Medium was added to thin out color. When toned in this way, the canvas takes time to dry so I prepared it in advance.

This free application allows for exciting variations of color and value, some of which are retained in your final painting. After this application is dry, I sketch in the composition, using a round sable or bristle brush and Ivory Black thinned with turpentine.

2. With the major lines of the composition indicated, the main areas of color and the value pattern were introduced. The entire canvas—sky, middle ground, foreground—was worked on at this stage rather than any one spot.

3. I allowed the original preparation to come through where it was effective. The next step introduced some details of houses, trees, walls, and paths; clarified shapes, intensified colors, and darkened or lightened areas to create depth.

Watch your source of light on objects and look for patterns or shapes in fields of grass. In this painting the greens were varied by mixing Thalo Green and Green Earth with a variety of colors such as Raw Sienna, Lemon Yellow, Burnt Sienna, and Thalo Blue (mixed with Thalo Green for a slightly colder color note than the Thalo Green alone). In most cases white was used as part of the mixtures. Grumbacher Transparent Brown was glazed over the foreground wall, again mixed with other colors to keep variety and interest in this area. Experiment with the exciting possibilities for color variety by mixing different combinations. Try more of an impasto application in the lightest areas.

2

3

PALETTE KNIFE

SPONGE

BROAD BRUSH

SMALL BRUSH

CRUMPLED CLOTH
DIPPED INTO PAINT
AND APPLIED TO SURFACE

PRESSING TECHNIQUE

SCRUBBING TECHNIQUE

To create interesting textures consider all the possibilities for applying paint. The painting knife or palette knife can, of course, be used in a variety of ways. In addition, vary the manner in which the brush is used and try a sponge, cloth, paper, or the pressing technique which produces exciting accidental effects. This technique consists of applying paint very thinly, in an almost creamy consistency, then pressing a piece of scrap drawing paper against it. The texture left on the canvas by the paper taking off some of the wet paint is extremely interesting. It is very good for the texture of trees and terrain. With practice you will develop more control. After an area dries you can go over it and add more texture. These effects should be achieved in early stages with oil and combined to build-up large areas of texture. It is necessary to work on a flat surface; otherwise the paint will run and be difficult to control.

In the three black and white sketches shown, the concentration is on the barn in each case. The first barn sketch was done primarily with the palette knife. In number two with a combination of brush and knife, and in number three the pressing technique was used.

For final composition I decided on a detail of the first barn sketch, taking in the two silos and at the same time reversing them and changing the path and fencing. The steps leading to completion show the same approach as in the previous landscape. Most of this painting was done with the knife. The brush was used for detail.

1. Light Red (English Red, Light), Burnt Sienna, Thalo Blue, and white were used to get the overall toning I wanted as a ground for this painting. The color was applied to the canvas freely with a palette knife and mixed on the surface. Some medium was used to thin the paint slightly. When this was dry the composition was sketched in using a round bristle brush with Ivory Black thinned with turpentine.

2. The main areas of color and value were laid in, with the color applied generously. With this technique you can scrape and re-work anything that doesn't seem right. It is important to work boldly and directly. Cobalt Violet and Burnt Sienna both mixed with white, were used in the sky area. In the foreground greens I also used the highly opaque Chromium Oxide Green.

In finishing, shapes were clarified, darks and lights were manipulated to strengthen the pattern, and detail was added.

The greatest difficulty for the beginning painter is the handling of trees and greenery in the summer landscape. For this demonstration Albert Pucci has selected a subject with a large grouping of trees; the building is of secondary interest.

A number of detailed sketches of trees and interesting shrubs were made with a felt pen and water color Lamp Black. (For this you could also use ink washes.) From this first viewpoint several compositions were made moving trees around where necessary. Then other sketches were made from other positions to vary the viewpoint. Black and white oil color sketches can be made on inexpensive canvas grained papers available in pad form. With oil sketches the palette or painting knife is an excellent tool for quick indications of foliage; the brush is used later for detail.

Try to achieve as much value contrast as possible. Note the different values of greens—some trees appear lighter in color and value than others. While making these black and white sketches jot down the names of mixtures of color that you might use in painting. This helps you to remember the impression of the subject that most interested you.

1. Once you are satisfied with your composition, decide what color and what value of that color will be most dominant in the overall painting. In this demonstration olive green of a middle value was most dominant. Start with Green Earth, Raw Umber, and Permanent Green, Light with a touch of Cadmium Yellow, Light. Using a large painting knife apply all colors freely and directly to the canvas, mixing on the canvas to achieve a fresh vibrant underpainting. Leave the application quite impasto.

When the underpainting is sufficiently dry, sketch your subject on it with a round sable brush dipped in Ivory Black thinned with turpentine.

2. When the drawing is finished, start laying in your lighter colors—the sky (a mixture of Thalo Blue and Superba White with French Ultramarine Blue and white) and sunlight on the trees and ground (Cadmium Yellow, Light, Permanent Green, Light, Cadmium Orange) all with white and intermixed in different degrees for each variety shown. Remember to permit as much of the underpainting to come through as possible.

By dragging your palette knife or brush over the surface of the underpainting you hit the high points, leaving paint on them with the green underpainting coming through. This gives an exciting textural quality and vibrancy to your painting.

84]

Draw with the side of the knife as well as the tip or flat portion. The flexible blade, can be used to apply paint in an infinite variety of lines and textures.

Color on a bristle brush was drawn across the tree horizontally after the trunk was indicated vertically with a palette knife.

The textural effects shown on page 86 were achieved solely by the use of a palette knife and a flat bristle brush. Before starting to paint the following snow scene, I prepared the entire canvas with an overall tone of middle gray or gray blue (white and French Ultramarine Blue with a touch of Burnt Sienna). Then with the palette knife I proceeded to put in patterns of snow, trees, etc. This page shows three different compositions. Again, in all three sketches the first step was to prepare the entire surface with an overall tone. The snow pattern was put in directly with the painting knife, as were the buildings and trees against this middle value of color.

Look for the whitest white and compare this to shadow tones or the medium light tones. Shadows are never too dark on snow-covered fields. Shadows are darker in late afternoon with a strong setting sun.

In addition to the painting knife or palette knife, vary the manner in which the brush is used, and experiment with other materials as well. Try a sponge, cloth, paper, or anything that might seem appropriate for applying paint and creating exciting textures.

An interesting technique for these accidental effects is the pressing technique. This consists of applying paint in an almost creamy consistency, then pressing a piece of scrap drawing paper against it. The texture left on the canvas by the paper taking off some of the wet paint is extremely interesting. It is very good for the texture to be found in terrain. With practice you will develop control. After an area dries you can go over it and add more texture. A very good manner for treating large areas to keep them interesting.

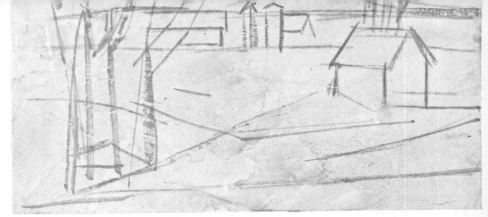

1

1. Prepare canvas with an overall tone, as in the sketch stage previously discussed. This should be of middle value, usually a bluish gray (a mixture of French Ultramarine Blue, Burnt Sienna and white) or Cerulean Blue, Cobalt Blue, a little French Ultramarine Blue, enough white and a bit of Ivory Black. In this case mix on the palette but not too thoroughly. This underpainting should be allowed to dry sufficiently to permit you to draw your subject on it.

   Sketch in the composition with a brush dipped in a thinned-out cobalt blue (see step 1).

2. Start to apply snow patterns with a palette knife. Some of your sketch will be obliterated as you do this but enough will remain to show location of subjects. Always be conscious of drawing as well as painting. One cannot exist without the other. Should you accidentally paint out areas already solved, don't panic! It is easy enough to re-cover the area by scraping off with the knife and restoring detail with a brush. Leave detail of trees and foreground till last.

3. Develop the dark masses of the buildings and tree trunk in the foreground. This is a combination of many colors in the finished painting, but is started with Burnt Sienna, Thalo Blue, and a touch of Alizarin Crimson mixed with a little white. The yellower browns of the buildings are a mixture of Burnt Sienna and Yellow Ochre with a touch of Thalo Green, again with white.

   The problem of the snow should be solved first, obviously, because it would be impossible to paint it between branches.

   Look over your painting—correct shapes, push darks darker if necessary, add more white with knife to trees, roof tops, etc.

   Put the painting aside for a few days, then come back to it. You may see things to change—either color or tones. Be daring and free.

2

3

1

2

John Grabach, ANA, an extremely versatile and well known artist, is noted for his beautiful textural landscapes as well as for seascapes and portraits. These other aspects of his work may be seen on pages 122-125 and 134-137.

The four preliminary drawings were made in preparation for the finished painting shown on the opposite page along with details.

In sketch number one the composition was judged too low with too little focus on the working figure. In number two the composition was considered too high and too far to the right, with not enough room for the eye to move around the main house and back into the painting. Number three was rejected because he felt it still lacked sufficient impact. Number four, selected for painting, leads the eye to the working figure and by means of spatial perspective permits the eye to move around the center of interest and back into the painting.

3

4

In the detail on the left (at bottom) can be seen the simplicity yet certainty with which the figure has been indicated. There is no attempt to labor over it; it is kept rather direct and in context with the painting as a whole. Details can be lost, and indeed would be better lost, to maintain an overall feeling in the painting.

This painting demonstrates the great variety of texture possible because of the way the ground is prepared. The ground is MG®

White, a fast-drying white made for this purpose. Color is brushed on, or scrubbed on in some cases, almost dry over the broad rough strokes of the white ground to produce an extremely rich surface texture. The detail on the right points up some of the quick, direct indication of trees made very simply with the wooden handle of the brush.

The problem in developing the composition of the "Lone House" was essentially the anchoring of a rectangular block floating in the air in the center of the canvas. This was solved by running lines on the horizontal plane, holding the house firmly in place and giving proper support to the composition.

1. A careful charcoal drawing was made directly on the canvas and sprayed with fixative.

2. The dark shadow patterns were painted in first with Thalo Blue and a small amount of Burnt Sienna.

3. In the next step Raw Sienna was used with a small amount of Zinc White. Viridian with some Yellow Ochre was used in the green sections and some Lemon Yellow was added to increase the intensity of the green.

The final painting employs the full range of a palette
consisting of:

Zinc White
Cadmium Yellow, Pale
Raw Sienna
Burnt Sienna
Thalo Blue
Yellow Ochre
Lemon Yellow

Cobalt Violet
Rose Madder
Indian Red
Viridian

SEASCAPE

Christopher Davis discusses approaches to drawing and painting along the waterfront through page 105.

The value of constant observation and sketching cannot be over emphasized. Before attempting to paint any subject, devote some time to drawing and composing its elements. Sketches assist in organizing the composition and lend authority to the details in your painting.

With the infinite variety of subject matter available to the painter along the waterfront it is important to analyze, select, examine forms and textures and eliminate or re-arrange for the best expression of the subject involved. The play of dark against light or texture against texture can be the means of keeping variety and interest in your paintings.

A thorough awareness of the underlying basic form of the subject makes it possible to combine successfully elements from var-

ious sketches. This will also alert you to patterns created by cast shadows and the "mood" possibilities within the subject as the result of changes in lighting. Move around the subject checking it in its simplest terms. Make many thumbnail sketches of the broad masses before going to anything more ambitious. When time is limited or painting materials are not available, don't hesitate to write color notes over your black and white sketches. These will recall the mood and general color of the subject with surprising accuracy.

As soon as you are satisfied with the over all composition make more detailed studies of the textures and other specifics of the subject. This procedure can be the means of saving you much time and grief when you start to paint.

1

2

3

In drawing (1) the eye is led into the composition by using the forms of the beach. Interest is kept in the grass by making it a dark mass against the sky.

Drawing (2) concentrates on the major form of the sailboat and plays light against dark with other forms in a manner that doesn't interfere with the primary statement.

In drawing (3) elements of the composition are unified by concentrating detail in the mass of shacks and the pier while background material is kept simple and understated.

The sky and a dark stain the color of the forms in the sand were put down with a brush. The palette knife was used to put in the lighter values in the sand and the deep greens of the grass. While the paint was still wet the edge of the knife was used to scrape away the light color and expose the darker underpainting for the form in the sand. The grass was painted with the edge of the knife.

The fishing shack was massed in as a dark form in the underpainting. When this was dry the grays of the building were painted, scraping away with the painting knife produced a variety of textures. Lines drawn through the wet paint with the knife and end of the brush exposed the underpainting for the edges of shingles on the roof and boards of the shack.

Rock forms should be painted with care to avoid lumpy, formless masses. Work out the pattern of darks adding lighter values within these darks suggesting reflected light and additional form. *The lighter values within the dark area should always be darker than the darkest value within the light area.* In this way the pattern and contrast of basic values originally painted can be maintained. The contrast of colors of uniform value within the dark and light areas will add interest as well as accentuate form. Water running around rocks follows the shape of the rock until it eddies out into open. The direction and pattern of this flow is an important aspect of your seascapes and should be carefully observed and sketched before starting to paint.

Old hulls with their peeling paint always present interesting subject matter. The following demonstration is one in which Christopher Davis uses a different approach to toning the canvas and a great deal of underpainting, scraping, repainting, and glazing to build up textural effects.

The painting was done in the studio from a number of felt pen drawings and snapshots taken on the spot to provide necessary detail. For most artists, snapshots themselves become meaningless after several months unless they are accompanied by sketches that serve as reminders of what was interesting about the subject in the first place.

The palette consisted of Flake White; Cadmium Yellow, Light; Yellow Ochre; Cadmium Red, Light; Burnt Sienna; English Red; French Ultramarine Blue; Thalo Blue; Viridian; and Cobalt Violet. Mixed with other colors, Cobalt Violet provides a range of interesting warm blues and grays; it also adds a good color note on its own.

1. After a series of smaller drawings and thumbnail roughs to decide on composition, a large drawing made with water color felt pen was prepared to the size of the finished painting. This was still quite rough but developed some of the pattern. Smaller drawings, from a combination of two or three sketches of the subject, supplied the detail to be brought in as the painting developed. At this stage the important thing was the broad pattern; most of the final drawing was done later with the brush and the palette knife on the canvas.

2. The drawing was transferred to the canvas and sprayed with fixative. The ground tone of the canvas was a wash of Thalo Blue and Cobalt Violet thinned with turpentine. The masses of the composition and the drawing were then strengthened with a mixture of Thalo Blue and Burnt Umber. The sky area (Thalo Blue,

Cobalt Violet and white) was then put in with a palette knife. The ground tone picked up in the color being applied made for an interesting effect.

3. An underpainting of the masses of the boat and foreground were also put in primarily with a palette knife. A great deal of scraping and reworking brought out the desired texture and shapes. This is the sort of thing that should be allowed for in the painting. Preplanning can and should be done only to a certain point.

4. Although all of the painting was developed and brought along at the same time, the final touch was the lightest grass in front of the boats. This was put in quickly with a palette knife. Anything that didn't seem right was simply scraped off, since the underpainting was already dry.

1

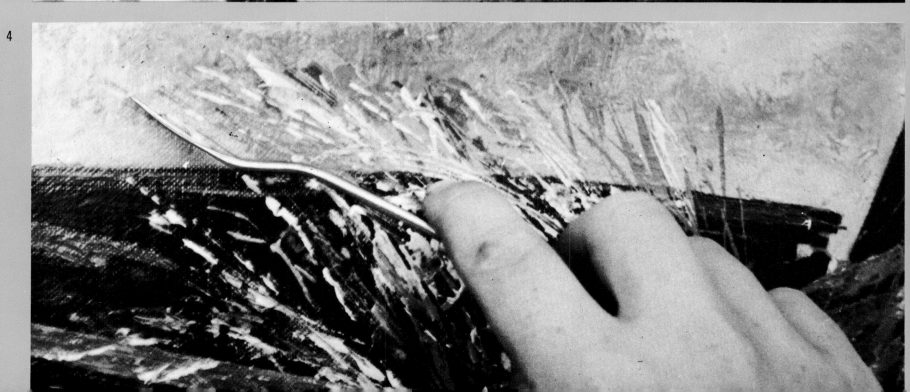

The painting was worked on over a period of time. Paint which had dried from the previous session was glazed making for an additional range of textures and modification of color beyond these achieved by working directly. This glazing, some of which is evident on the lower portion of the foreground boat, consists of brushing on diluted washes of color using a sable brush. In other instances, as in the lower left corner area between the boats, color was applied quite dry. This is called scumbling. Massing in the composition in the manner described on the previous pages makes it easier to keep the various values in their proper relationship. By establishing a middle value of color on the overall canvas it is possible to work up to the lightest values in the

light areas, and with the drawing as a guide, keep everything from the middle value to black within the dark areas.

A small knife was used to paint the stalks of grass and for scraping and building up textures in small areas. The end of a brush handle served to draw the lines of planking on the foreground boat as well as other wood textures while paint was wet. The underpainting was permitted to show through to give the lines the desired color.

The following demonstration by Christopher Davis introduces an interesting approach that utilizes a fast-drying under painting to permit almost immediate over-painting with oils.

There is no subject area richer in pattern and texture for the landscape painter than the boatyard and waterfront.

In the jumble usually characteristic of such scenes, it is important to learn to be selective. By half closing your eyes and squinting you will eliminate the bulk of minor detail and see only the essential pattern. This observation and drawing will develop a personal sense of picture arrangement, which is one of the most important parts of painting.

The camera is a useful tool for recording detail, but snapshots themselves are rather meaningless when reviewed some months later unless they are accompanied by sketches to remind you of what originally interested you in the subject. Gathering material by sketching has the added value of recreating a much clearer visual image for you of the subject's mood, color, and effect.

The drawing to the right is a felt-pen rough (done to size of the final painting) for composition and arrangement of the color demonstration on the following pages.

The subject was painted on pressed wood prepared with Hyplar® Gesso. This gesso, an acrylic polymer (see page 182) is an excellent ground for oil and can be used to surface canvas, plywood, pressed wood, cardboard, or any other non-oil surface. Underpainting colors were Hyplar polymer and oils were used for the finish. Acrylic colors are extremely fast drying and permit a rapid completion of preliminary work.

1. The entire surface is covered with a middle value warm blue (Thalo Blue and Grumbacher Purple) and the drawing sketched in Mars Black. Polymer is used because it is so fast drying and makes an excellent base for the oil.

2. The color areas of the overpainting are executed in oil with the painting knife, scraping and rescraping to build up desired textures. Small areas are applied with either a smaller knife or brush.

Plan your painting only up to a certain point. Allow for exciting things that can happen as you develop the various areas. Look for interesting "accidents" in color and texture as you get into the final stages.

The oil color palette used was Zinc White, Cadmium Yellow, Light, Yellow Ochre, Thalo Blue, Viridian, Burnt Sienna, Alizarin Crimson, and Cobalt Violet.

As the color is put in a certain amount of drawing as well as texture is established by scraping it out again, as is illustrated by the water area. The texture and masses in the sky and various color areas of the boat were finally developed by a combination of glazing (putting thin washes of color over areas that have dried to subdue or accent them) and scumbling (applying a dryer pigment—almost as it comes from the tube—so that it brushes off on the surface letting underpainting come through).

1

2

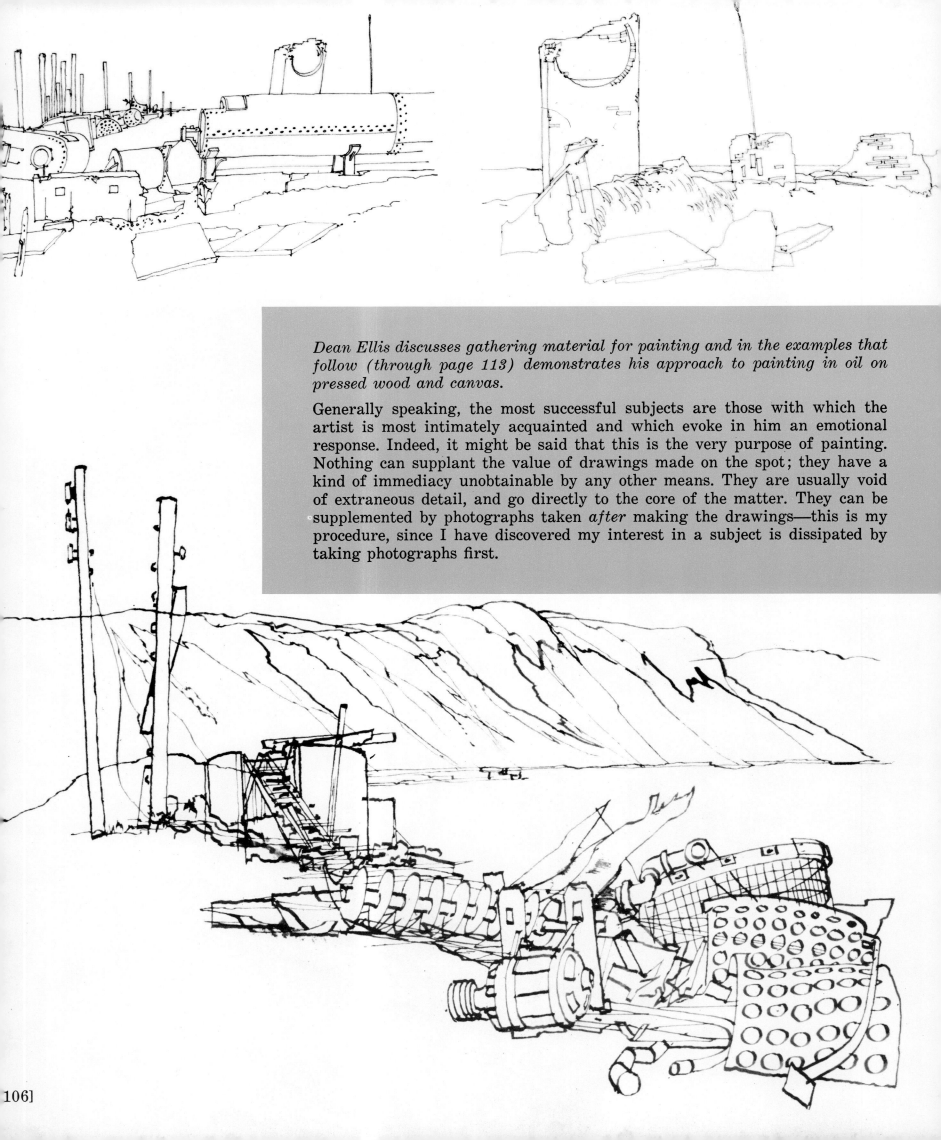

Dean Ellis discusses gathering material for painting and in the examples that follow (through page 113) demonstrates his approach to painting in oil on pressed wood and canvas.

Generally speaking, the most successful subjects are those with which the artist is most intimately acquainted and which evoke in him an emotional response. Indeed, it might be said that this is the very purpose of painting. Nothing can supplant the value of drawings made on the spot; they have a kind of immediacy unobtainable by any other means. They are usually void of extraneous detail, and go directly to the core of the matter. They can be supplemented by photographs taken *after* making the drawings—this is my procedure, since I have discovered my interest in a subject is dissipated by taking photographs first.

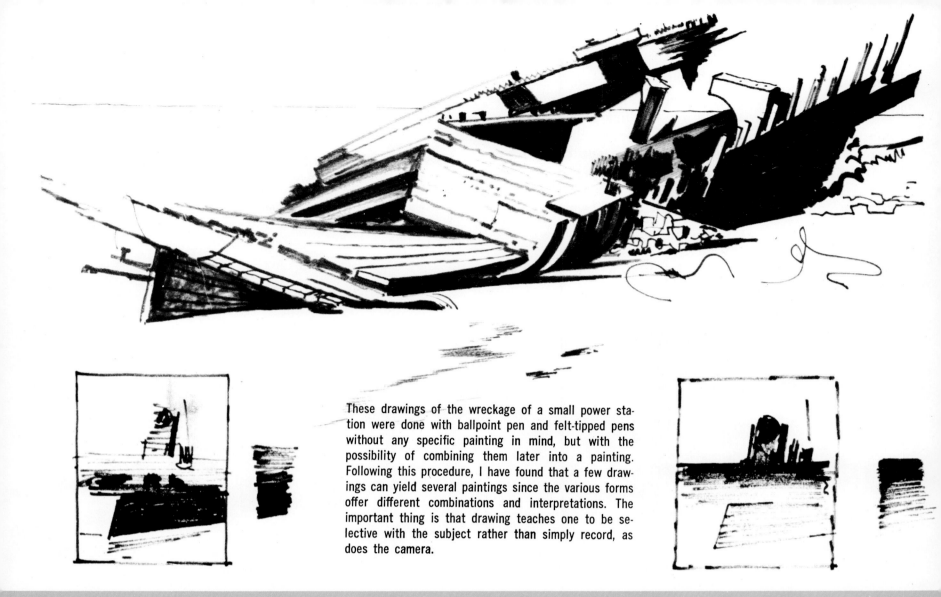

These drawings of the wreckage of a small power station were done with ballpoint pen and felt-tipped pens without any specific painting in mind, but with the possibility of combining them later into a painting. Following this procedure, I have found that a few drawings can yield several paintings since the various forms offer different combinations and interpretations. The important thing is that drawing teaches one to be selective with the subject rather than simply record, as does the camera.

I usually make compositional notes such as these before I begin painting. They serve to explore the placement of various elements within the selected format and as experiments with the massing of lights and darks —all with the ultimate purpose of achieving various interpretations. It is important to mention the desirability of retaining flexibility at this stage and of not freezing one's thinking too early, since room should be left for spontaneous improvisation during the painting.

This painting was executed on a pressed wood panel that had been prepared with Hyplar Gesso brushed on with a large three-inch brush. The brush marks were allowed to stand, and a very dark ground tone composed of Ivory Black and Cobalt Blue, was spread over the surface. When this was dry, the principal elements and masses were roughly indicated with light pastel, which was sprayed with fixative, and the painting begun.

Working with a palette consisting of Flake White; Ivory Black; Burnt Umber; Raw Umber; Yellow Ochre; Cadmium Orange; Alizarin Crimson Golden; Cadmium Red, Light; Cobalt Blue; and Thalo Green; I laid in the sky with a palette knife. This surface was then alternately scraped with the knife and brushed with a flat sable brush to provide some subtle variety and depth of texture.

Next the principal light masses were put down with a palette knife, but they were not as light as I ultimately intended. The same was done with the darks,

keeping them lighter than they would eventually be. In other words, at this stage the values were in less contrast than I intended them to be when finished.

When this stage was thoroughly dry, broad glazes were brushed across the sky and dark areas of the painting. These consisted of Burnt Umber and Alizarin Crimson Golden in a glazing medium; while still tacky they were further worked over with a rag and scraped with a knife. The whole purpose was to achieve a dramatic progression of light across the painting from left to right, to set the mood. Then the light areas were again worked on, this time with heavier paint and lighter values. Considerable attention was paid to edges where light areas met dark. Finally, details were added with small sable brushes and the edges of painting knives and final touches and accents of the lightest lights and darkest darks were put down—these last at the extremes of the value scale within the tonality of the painting.

Becoming familiar with the subject can't be stressed enough. Familiarity, the result of observation and drawing, comes through in the final painting as well as in the initial drawing with an authority that can be obtained in no other way. A combination of many such drawings as shown on these pages, has become the painting in the following demonstration — and by re-emphasis and re-arrangement can become the source for many additional paintings.

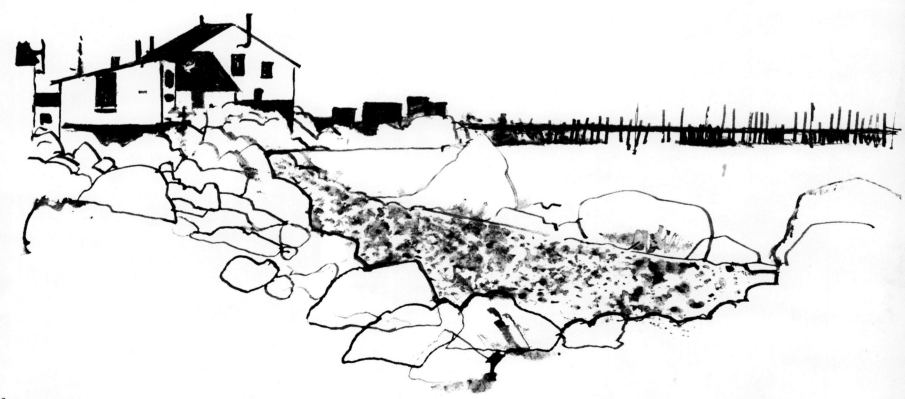

Distant objects light, foreground dark.

Don't hesitate to experiment with value arrangements of the subject matter as shown here.

Lights in distance, sky and foreground dark.

Light from an unidentified unexplained source above creates a mood of mystery and increases interest in subject . . . foreground light.

1. This painting was executed over a previously prepared canvas painted with a mixture of Ivory Black and Cobalt Blue. After the ground was dry, the principal elements and masses were roughly indicated with light pastel and the painting was begun.

2. The sky, a mixture of Cobalt Blue and Superba White with a touch of Burnt Sienna to gray it, was laid in with a palette knife, and this surface was alternately scraped down and repainted to allow the texture of the canvas to come through.

3. Next the principal light masses were put down with a palette knife, but not as light as I ultimately intended them to be. The same was done with the darks, keeping them lighter than they would eventually be. In other words, at this stage the values were less contrasting than I intended them to be when the painting was finished. For the foreground a mixture of Yellow Ochre and white was used. The greens are Chromium Oxide Green with Yellow Ochre and white.

When the previous stage was thoroughly dry, broad glazes were brushed into the rock mass and foreground as well as over the light strip of building on the horizon.

After this the light areas were again worked on, this time with heavier paint and lighter values. Considerable attention was paid to edges where light areas met dark. Finally, details were added with small brushes and the edge of the painting knife.

Final touches and accents of the lightest lights and darkest darks were put down, these last at the extremes of the value scale within the tonality of the painting.

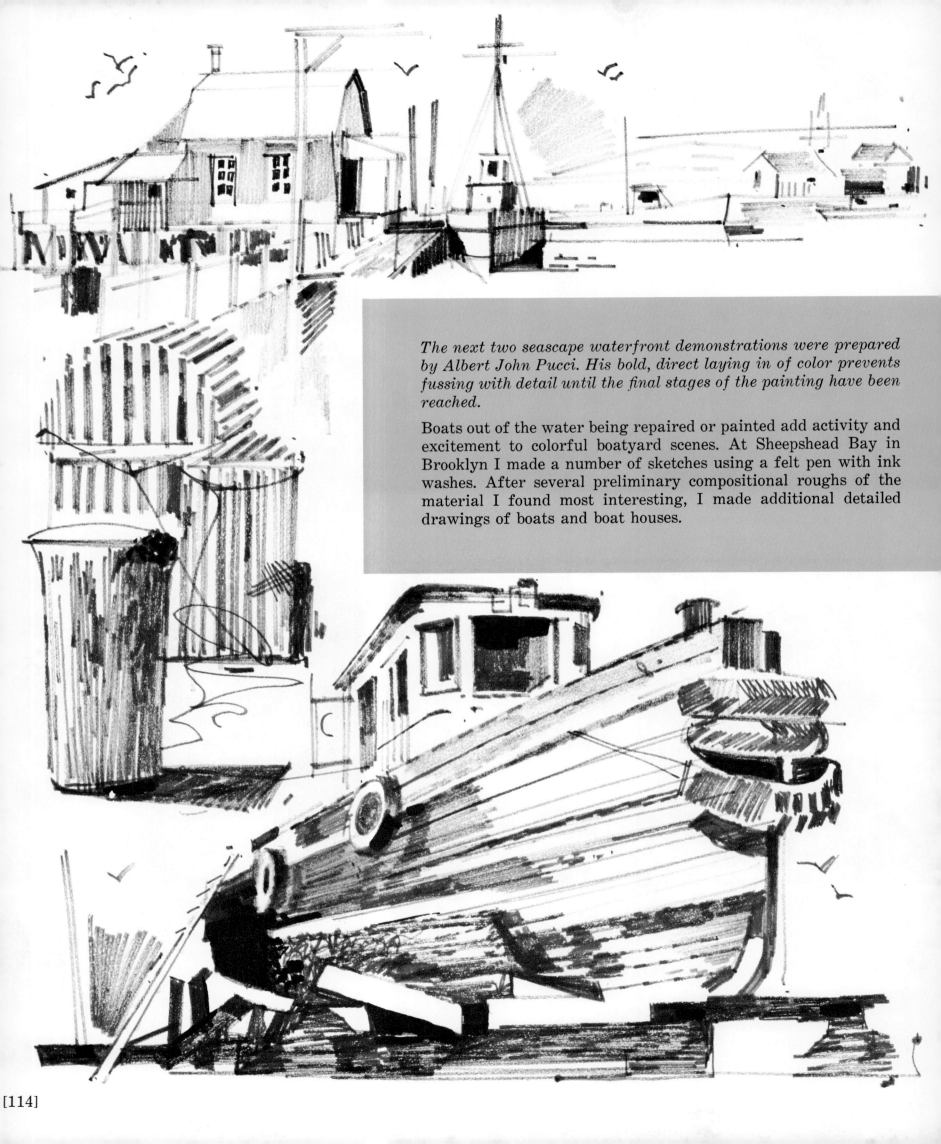

The next two seascape waterfront demonstrations were prepared by Albert John Pucci. His bold, direct laying in of color prevents fussing with detail until the final stages of the painting have been reached.

Boats out of the water being repaired or painted add activity and excitement to colorful boatyard scenes. At Sheepshead Bay in Brooklyn I made a number of sketches using a felt pen with ink washes. After several preliminary compositional roughs of the material I found most interesting, I made additional detailed drawings of boats and boat houses.

Back in my studio I re-arranged elements to suit my final composition, even, where necessary, changing perspective slightly for a more dramatic effect. I then proceeded to prepare my canvas for painting. Noting that most of the subject was dark I decided to cover the canvas with a color of rich dark reddish browns. This was done with Burnt Sienna; Burnt Umber; English Red; Light; and Ivory Black. I applied these colors to my canvas with a painting knife, knifing freely enough to achieve a certain amount of texture. By applying these colors as they were put on the palette (full intensity) one against the other, rather than mixing on the palette, I find that I get a much more interesting underpainting to work into and can take advantage in the later painting of the exciting "accidents" that come about in the relationship of colors. I allowed this ground to dry then with turpentine thinned color drew in my composition using a round sable brush.

I proceeded with the painting knife to lay in relatively middle value sky tones to silhouette the large shapes, boat, boathouse, etc. Other values were held low in key keeping the lighter values for the final stages. I then put color into the foreground areas allowing much of the ground color to remain. With the textured ground it is possible to apply color holding the knife very flat so that color hits the raised areas only. This makes for an exciting blend of ground color showing through the lighter or darker colors being applied.

When all of the large masses were completed in this manner I used a bristle brush for detailing and putting in whatever linear quality was necessary. This might also have been done with a painting knife if a freer result was desired. At this stage the brightest areas were brought up and dark accents put in where necessary.

My palette for painting this subject was as follows:

Titanium White
Cadmium Yellow, Light
Yellow Ochre
Raw Sienna
English Red, Light

Burnt Sienna
Burnt Umber
Cerulean Blue
Ivory Black

Before starting to sketch I walked around this exciting place to study it from various viewpoints. When I was satisfied with this scrutiny I made a series of quick sketches of the lighthouse, dunes, rocks, surf, etc.

The lighthouse area alone was enough for a good painting but after walking along the beach, I decided on a long view which included much of the surrounding land plus water, beach, lighthouse and sky. It was late summer so the grass had many browns through it, and the patchy clouds made an exciting play of light and dark which I accented into a strong pattern.

This painting was done in my studio from the material gathered on my trip. I had noted the deep color in the shadows of the grasses and rocks and decided to work on a Burnt Umber ground. Umbers dry rapidly so, in this instance, the canvas was ready for overpainting the following day. A dark foundation color allows me to achieve a vibrant response when applying lighter and brighter colors. The dark color coming through makes for interesting textural effects as well.

1. I sketched in my composition with Thalo Blue mixed with white and thinned with turpentine —using a round sable brush.

2. Next I blocked in my large sky areas and water masses using a painting knife. The palette for this was as follows: Superba White; Thalo Blue; Ultramarine Blue; Raw Umber and Ivory Black. White was used with each color to keep it all within a desired value range. In this manner it was possible to get interesting changes of color and still have the areas hold together as a unit.

3. In the land areas I used Grumbacher Permanent Bright Green; Raw Sienna; Green Earth; Cadmium Yellow, Medium; Cadmium Red, Light; Superba White and Ivory Black. Rather than risk overmixing colors on the palette I applied them as directly as possible and let them blend on the canvas.

Lightest and brightest accents were put in last. In addition to the painting knife, I used bristle and sable brushes to suggest rather than elaborate for details.

The roughs on this page, in watercolor, felt pen, and charcoal, are typical of the studies that John Grabach, ANA makes before starting to paint. In this demonstration he works out the broad masses of his composition so that when painting in oils he can be more direct. Mr. Grabach's capable brush handling and very direct method of painting makes an excellent approach to painting on the spot. His work is in many public and private collections.

The painting of a fine marine is a rewarding experience. The subject itself is an unusual challenge because of the constant motion of the sea. You must be able to capture the excitement of a pounding surf, the depth, the weight, and even the saltiness of the sea; the feeling of movement in wind and water, as opposed to the solidity and immobility of the rocks. Incorporate all of this into a strong composition and you will be entirely deserving of that feeling of tremendous accomplishment.

Before setting out with equipment in hand it might be well to consider some of the unique problems encountered in painting a marine. The surf may not be rough or rolling in beautifully on the day you decide to paint it. You may have to wait for an off-shore wind as well as an incoming tide. In midsummer when the rocks reflect unbearable heat try to restrict yourself to the cooler morning or evening hours. Even in comfortable weather avoid the midday sun which destroys your shadows. You'll find the sea at its roughest just before or after a storm when the winds are usually strong. A large canvas makes a wonderful sail so your easel must be well anchored. I find the combination sketch box-easel is well worth its higher price under such conditions. It is sturdy and strong, and when closed makes a compact carrying case for paints, brushes, palette, and canvas, a convenience doubly appreciated if you have to walk any distance to your subject. The opened easel also holds the palette while you're painting, and a rock placed on the box provides extra insurance in the stiffest breeze. Setting the length of each leg to accommodate your rocky perch is also an easy adjustment with this easel. And now that we're all set to paint—remember one more thing—*Look before you step back* to view that painting.

The preliminary sketch for the following seascape was done directly with a felt pen on my sketch pad.
Speed is necessary to catch the constant movement when drawing surf.

Start with a charcoal drawing directly on the canvas. Get the rhythm of the line in your composition. Carefully observe the breaking waves. Keep the rocks and surf in a pleasing arrangement. Notice the pattern that takes place before the water breaks over. Keep the rocks square and sharp.

1. Paint the dark masses in the rocks first. Use Prussian Blue with Burnt Sienna and a small amount of Raw Sienna with Zinc White. For the light part of the rocks use Burnt Sienna, a little Raw Sienna, a small amount of Ultramarine Violet, and Zinc White. The medium is Linseed Oil and the brushes are bristle Flat and Brights. Your brush strokes should always follow the form and planes of the rocks.

2. There is unceasing movement in water. Paint in as quickly as possible with a fully loaded brush in a direct manner. First lay in the essential dark masses, then the light masses. Use a small amount of medium.

For both the dark and light masses in the water my palette consists of the following colors in varying proportions: Viridian; Raw Sienna; Ultramarine Violet, and Zinc White.

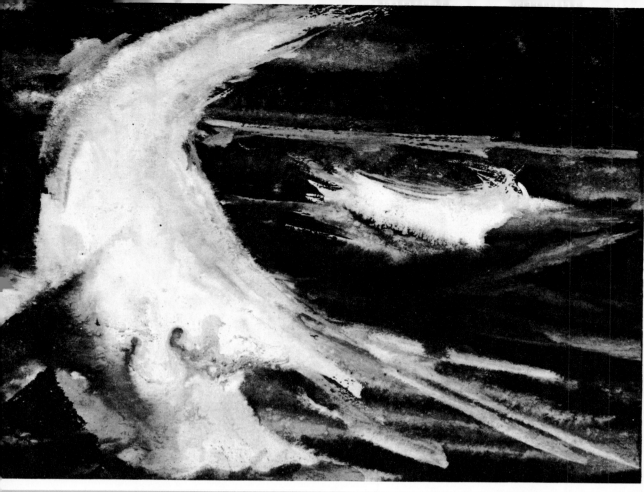

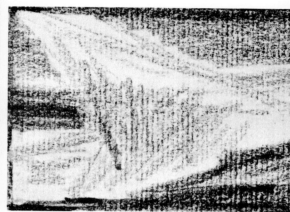

The next two demonstrations (through page 133) were prepared by Richard Gorman Powers. Mr. Powers' work has been shown at the Museum of Modern Art in N.Y.C. and he is represented in many public as well as private collections. (He shows at the Rehn Gallery in N.Y.C.)

Even though a painter prefers to work in a more or less non-literal, abstract idiom, out-of-door sketching is still essential if he is concerned with producing solid work with real body to it. This out-of-doors painting in the case of an abstractionist has as its purpose not the production of attractive sketches from nature, but the acquisition of authentic material in the form of direct experience, and of analytical studies done on the spot for use later in the studio. It is best to spend the time when working out-of-doors in observing what actually happens and making accurate analytical studies rather than trying abstractions on the spot. Particularly in marine painting, working conditions are likely to be rugged. Unfortunately, perhaps, the most rewarding and dramatic effects where the ocean is concerned generally take place with high winds, cold, flung spray or driving rain. Under these circumstances, prepare to work *fast* and *safe*. Make small monochromatic studies in safe non-smudging techniques before essaying the color study. Carry a plastic bottle of ink wash, Conté crayon, felt pen, etc. Anchor the easel with a strong cord (oiled fisherman's-net cord is best); be sure to observe high tide marks and keep well above them. And to stress a matter rather more important to the abstractionist than is generally acknowledged, when working from nature, study and analyze with a little humility. One can get even with, or better still top nature, in the privacy of the studio. The more diligent and analytical the out-of-doors working habits, the more naturalistic detail and atmosphere the painter makes part of his experience, the more solid *substance* (as opposed to representational *subject matter*) the abstraction will have. Be tough with yourself out-of-doors, be tough on the painting in the studio.

Take a wave form from one outdoor sketch, a rock formation from another, an atmospheric detail from another (midmorning fog in this painting). Put them together and they provide enough material for a proper studio painting.

Build on a strong foundation; strong forms, bold outlines, strong color. If there is plenty of strength at the start, it will still be there under the surface of the finished painting, no matter how subtle and/or complicated the final effect.

In contrast to the technique employed for the abstract marine still life (following pages) it is best to work as loosely and yet as powerfully as possible on seascapes. Deliberately work in and out of form, back and forth as it were, establishing forms and obliterating them with overlying structure (the white foam forms in the waves, for example): Lay in the base green and gray-green (Grumbacher Permanent Bright Green; Chromium Oxide Green; and Superba White) of the wave form; drag a middle foam gray

(Raw Umber; Ultramarine Blue and white) over it in the spray patterns. Wash more green over the gray, come back with a lighter value of the foam gray, work in an area of kelp and sea-weed warm color (Cadmium Red, Deep; Raw Umber and white) and overpaint with the foam gray. Use the painting knife to slash in spray highlights (white and a touch of Raw Sienna, in sunlight, or, as in this painting, pure white) over the kelp area, back and forth, back and forth, somewhat in the very way waves form them-selves, subside and re-form. It is possible to build a great deal of movement into wave forms in this manner.

Save the knife work for the final stages, however. More painters have hurt themselves (figuratively speaking) with the painting knife than with any other of the artist's tools.

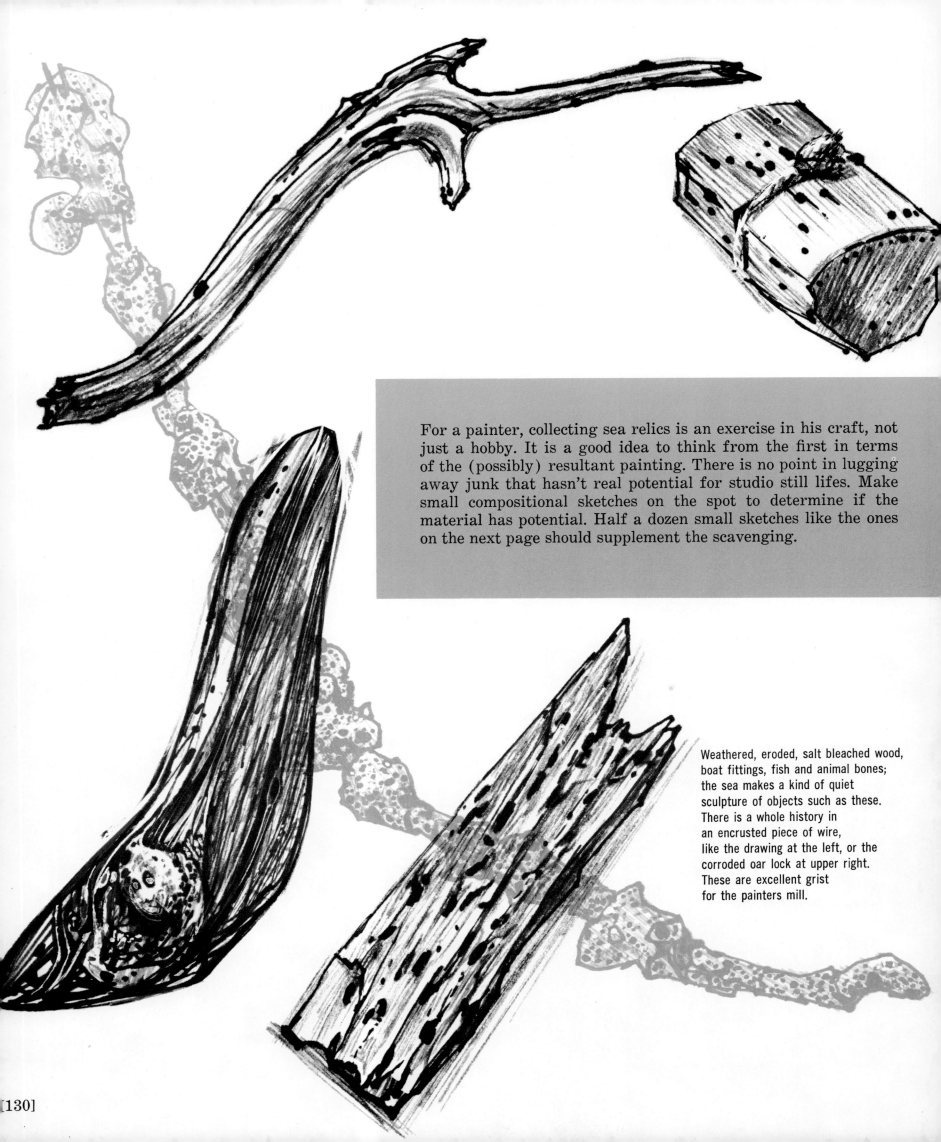

For a painter, collecting sea relics is an exercise in his craft, not just a hobby. It is a good idea to think from the first in terms of the (possibly) resultant painting. There is no point in lugging away junk that hasn't real potential for studio still lifes. Make small compositional sketches on the spot to determine if the material has potential. Half a dozen small sketches like the ones on the next page should supplement the scavenging.

Weathered, eroded, salt bleached wood, boat fittings, fish and animal bones; the sea makes a kind of quiet sculpture of objects such as these. There is a whole history in an encrusted piece of wire, like the drawing at the left, or the corroded oar lock at upper right. These are excellent grist for the painters mill.

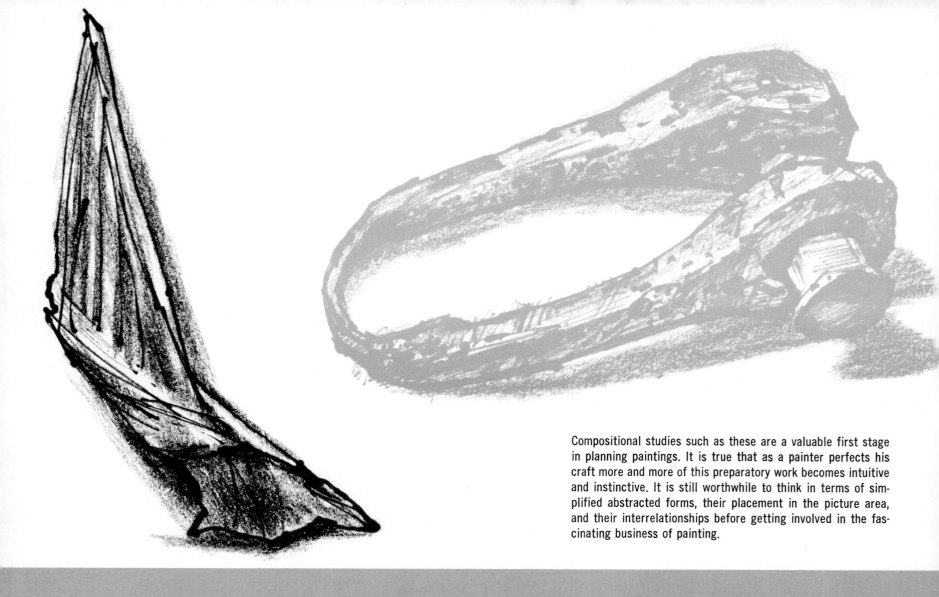

Compositional studies such as these are a valuable first stage in planning paintings. It is true that as a painter perfects his craft more and more of this preparatory work becomes intuitive and instinctive. It is still worthwhile to think in terms of simplified abstracted forms, their placement in the picture area, and their interrelationships before getting involved in the fascinating business of painting.

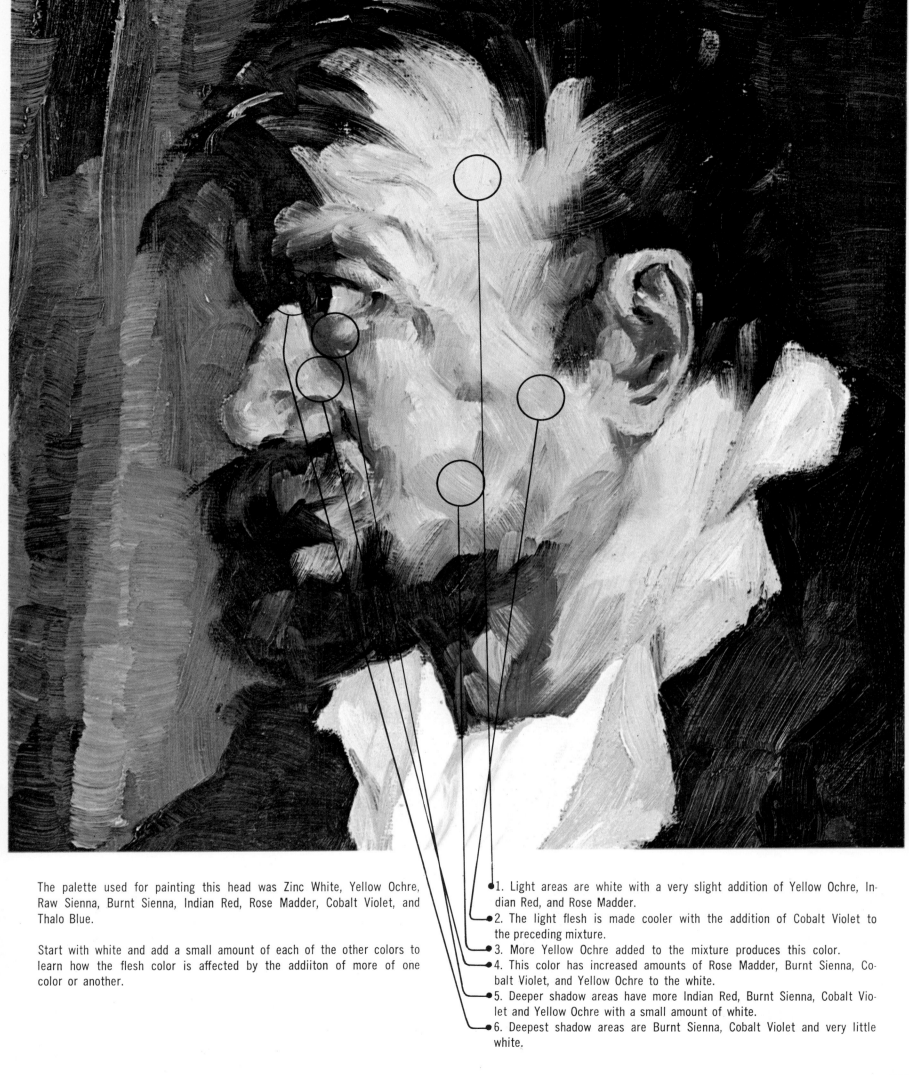

The palette used for painting this head was Zinc White, Yellow Ochre, Raw Sienna, Burnt Sienna, Indian Red, Rose Madder, Cobalt Violet, and Thalo Blue.

Start with white and add a small amount of each of the other colors to learn how the flesh color is affected by the addiiton of more of one color or another.

1. Light areas are white with a very slight addition of Yellow Ochre, Indian Red, and Rose Madder.

2. The light flesh is made cooler with the addition of Cobalt Violet to the preceding mixture.

3. More Yellow Ochre added to the mixture produces this color.

4. This color has increased amounts of Rose Madder, Burnt Sienna, Cobalt Violet, and Yellow Ochre to the white.

5. Deeper shadow areas have more Indian Red, Burnt Sienna, Cobalt Violet and Yellow Ochre with a small amount of white.

6. Deepest shadow areas are Burnt Sienna, Cobalt Violet and very little white.

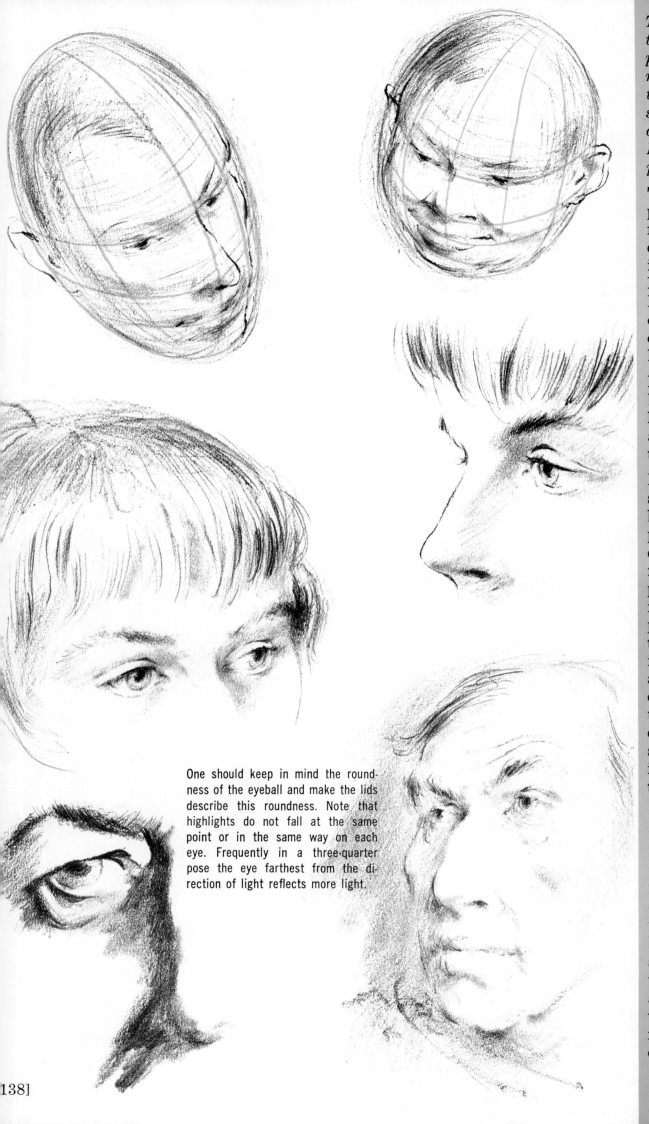

One should keep in mind the roundness of the eyeball and make the lids
describe this roundness. Note that
highlights do not fall at the same
point or in the same way on each
eye. Frequently in a three-quarter
pose the eye farthest from the direction of light reflects more light.

*The following portrait demonstra-
tions (through page 144) were
prepared by Lawrence Beal Smith,
noted American painter and illustrator. Mr. Smith is extremely versatile and is known for landscapes
as well as all phases of portraiture.
He is unsurpassed in his sensitive
portrayal of children.*

The basic ingredient in all fine
portrait painting is drawing. Your
first step should be many studies
of your subject. The human head
is in simple terms an egg shape.
Lean or fat, we are all egg heads.
From this simple basic concept, we
can then proceed in stages to the
complex form that is the individual
human skull.

Lines drawn around the egg in
both directions can become guide
lines for placing eyes, mouth, nose,
and ears, as shown in the illustrations.

It is essential to have such an abstract framework to rely upon
because of the possible change in
position of the model and conse-
quently in what the eye sees in the
model from sitting to sitting. A
portrait would never be completed
if the painter were to alter his
painting with each change in position of his sitter. Each human head
is, of course, a form incorporating
all the related features, but the
eyes are frequently the key to both
total composition and mood. For
example, the character of some
subjects seems to demand a pose
in which the eyes look directly at
the painter.

In my opinion, a touch of carica-
ture is necessary in a good portrait.
The best portraits always have
this ingredient. Frequently the effort to exaggerate form, gesture,
or color produces something closer
to a sense of reality. Avoid very
heavy shadows. They tend to destroy form. Unless the drawing of
the head is structurally sound, no
amount of shading will increase
the feeling of three-dimensional
form. When strong light and shadow are used, keep the shadow areas

light in texture by applying the paint in thin washes. Dark colors lose their luminosity when applied thickly. Just the opposite is true for the light colors.

Although attention invariably centers on the head in a portrait, it should, in the complete portrait, be considered only one of the many elements contributing to the life and vitality of the painting. Each human body has its own character and proportions. Hands can be very important to the overall statement. Above all, the gesture of the figure, as related to the head, should be given close attention. It is possible even in a small portrait to suggest a person of delicate stature simply by the gesture of the head in relation to neck and shoulders.

With more of the figure included, the possibilities for pictorial composition are greatly increased. The placing of hands in relation to the head can contribute to pattern.

At all times, the placing of forms and their thrust should be considered in relation to the outside edges of the canvas. There is no formula for such relationships, but by keeping in mind not only the subject being painted but also the surrounding space, a sense of rightness can be achieved. This rightness should include both the flat pattern effect of the forms involved and the three-dimensional, spatial pattern as well.

It is advisable to use logic when painting the folds in clothing in view of the fact that they are constantly changing during the progress of repeated sittings. Unessential folds should be eliminated in favor of those which describe form and contribute to compositional rhythms.

It is helpful to think of arms, legs, and torso as simple cylinders, and to think of these cylinders thrusting into space on a central axis (see illustration).

Note the spatial diamond area established by the head, arms, and hands.

The neck also is a cylinder, and costumes can be used to describe this. It can be helpful to actually draw around these cylindrical forms to establish the "feel" of the unseen back curve.

To paint a child is to paint a moving target. The painter is forced to rely heavily upon not only what his eye sees during a specific sitting, but also what he knows to be the logic of form and gesture within the scale set by the age and physical development of his subject.

Because the composition seemed clear to me there was no preliminary sketching for this painting. My decision was to maintain a simplicity in pattern and color. A light neutral background was used to dramatize the dark pattern of blouse, hair, and eyes.

In the painting of the head the simple egg form was established and the features were placed in relation to this form.

The hair color was first put down as a reddish brown, a mixture of Burnt Sienna and Alizarin Crimson, which acted as an underpainting for the darker tones which were to follow (see illustration below).

The luminous quality of the oil medium is achieved by the process of laying transparent glazes of one color over another. The color of the underpainting shows through the transparent glaze and one color modifies another. The underpainting should be at least partially, and preferably, completely dry before additional color is brushed over it. As a general rule it is a good procedure to work from a light base and from colors of greatest chromatic intensity toward modified neutral tones.

The soft hair line was established by painting flesh into hair and vice versa.

The pupils of the eyes were first set in as simple spots as in the sketch below. Darkening and details came later. Highlights, such as on forehead, cheeks, and chin, were placed as guide points at the same time as the features. Note that the flesh of the arms was painted up into the sleeve even though it will eventually be covered by the sleeve color.

The rhythms of the skirt folds were used to accentuate the circular rhythm of the arms and hands.

The hands were kept simple with only a suggested articulation of fingers.

My palette varies with each painting. In this instance it was very simple:

Superba White	Alizarin Crimson
Ivory Black	Mars Violet
Naples Yellow	Cerulean Blue
Yellow Ochre	Raw Umber
Raw Sienna	Burnt Umber
Burnt Sienna	French Ultramarine Blue
Cadmium Orange	Viridian
Cadmium Red, Light	

Lawrence Beall Smith

[141]

The full figure portrait increases the compositional challenge for the painter. It is not necessary to increase the size of the canvas. Such portraits can be done on a relatively small canvas.

Note the arbitrary repeated rhythms of the pigtail, the pull of drapery, and the branch in this figure. Hands are important in a portrait—try giving them something to do. Don't let them hang limp and lifeless.

There are endless possibilities for variety in the approach to a portrait head. Although each human

head has its own specific character, it should be understood that the best portraits are those which incorporate, in addition to the ephemeral thing called "likeness," the abstract elements of design, color, proportion, and scale which make for a satisfying picture.

It is sometimes helpful to consider the use of foils, such as flowers and headdresses, to give variety to design.

Sometimes the back of a head can be expressive of specific likeness as well (see top illustration).

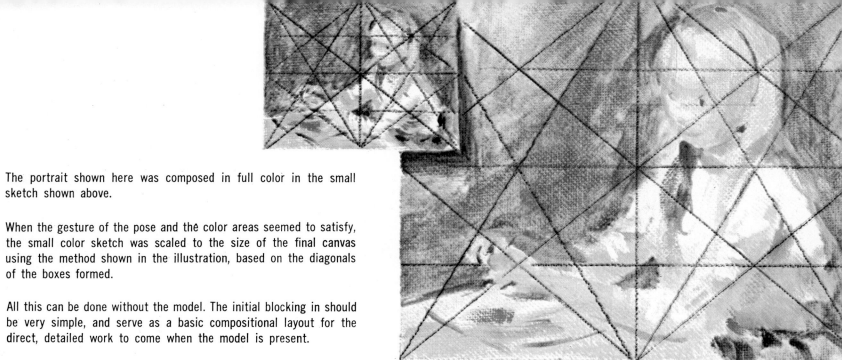

The portrait shown here was composed in full color in the small sketch shown above.

When the gesture of the pose and the color areas seemed to satisfy, the small color sketch was scaled to the size of the final canvas using the method shown in the illustration, based on the diagonals of the boxes formed.

All this can be done without the model. The initial blocking in should be very simple, and serve as a basic compositional layout for the direct, detailed work to come when the model is present.

WATERCOLOR

Donald Moss, a noted watercolorist whose works are shown both here and abroad demonstrates the subtle and delicate as well as the bold and dramatic possibilities of watercolor. As a medium it has a freshness and vitality which comes from the spontaneity with which it is handled. It does, however, demand great facility in brush handling and an understanding of the properties of pigments and paper surfaces.

MATERIAL

For your early attempts, a set like the one shown, should serve you well. You should select high quality brushes and paper, however, if you wish to obtain reasonably good results.

COLORS: Your basic palette (which comes with the set) should include:

Cadmium Yellow, Pale	Yellow Ochre
Grumbacher Red	Burnt Sienna
Alizarin Crimson	Burnt Umber
Light Red (English Red)	French Ultramarine Blue
Payne's Gray	Thalo® Blue
Cerulean Blue	Thalo® Green
Cobalt Blue	Ivory Black

BRUSHES: Buy the best brushes your budget permits, even if you have to start with just a few. With experience, you will want to add to your collection of brushes as well as experiment with additional color on your palette. A size 12 red sable brush is best for all around painting. For detail and smaller areas, you will need a size 3 and a size 8. A flat, red sable or ox hair brush such as the Grumbacher Aquarelle, in ¾" to 1" sizes is useful for laying in larger washes. In addition, these brushes come with a beveled end to the handle which is good for certain effects. Don't leave brushes standing in your water container after use. They should be rinsed with clear water, shaped and stored so that the hair does not come in contact with any surface.

PALETTE: A palette comes with the student set shown. When the tray is removed, both sides of the box can be used for mixing color. The larger CAPRI Palette shown opposite is extremely useful for painting on the spot. It closes up to a convenient carrying case for brushes and color.

PAPER: Watercolor paper comes in a variety of surfaces and weights. The principal textures are hot-pressed (HP), which has a very smooth finish; cold-pressed (CP), which has a slight texture; and rough finish (R), which has the most texture. On page 147 lower left, can be seen the textures of Capri (CP) and Rough (R) papers. The general size for sheets is 22" x 30" and papers range in weight from 72 lb. to 300 lb. The heavier weight papers (300 lb. and up) are generally most desirable because they buckle least when wet. For painting out of doors, there is a wide range of paper available in block and pad form. Mounted watercolor papers (boards) are also available.

ACCESSORIES: Many of the "tricks" in watercolor, as they are sometimes called, depend on additional tools such as blotters, sponges, razors, and masking materials. These should be added to your list along with a rag for wiping your brushes. Pencils for drawing in the subject should not be too hard or they will dig into the surface of the paper. For cleaning up pencil work from the finished painting, add a kneaded eraser to your equipment.

Capri 2121 CP

Capri 2121 R

Water Color Block

Here we show the different effects of two paper textures on the same subject. Cold-pressed paper was used on the left and on the right, a rough paper with more texture was used.

Watercolor should have a spontaneity and freshness. Any reworking of the painting has a tendency to destroy these qualities. It is a medium that requires experience and control. Develop your skills before starting to paint actual subjects by experimenting with effects to be obtained with strokes, washes, blotting, sponging, etc.

Flood water onto paper laid flat. Into this wash one color from one side and another color from the other. See how the colors "explode" or diffuse one into another. Tilt the paper to see what happens from different angles as washes run. Practice laying down graded washes by dampening the paper and, starting with a quantity of color in the brush, run a stroke across the top — dip the brush in clear water and overlap the first stroke with the second — keep

The sky is an example of a graded wash leaving the white of the paper to form the clouds. Hills were put in with a size 8 round sable while the sky was still slightly damp.

adding water with each stroke until the pigment blends out to the white of the paper.

Draw with the side of the brush. Blot the brush before applying to paper to examine dry brush effects. Pick up color from a wash with the edge of the blotter for the linear effects possible with this accessory.

The number of experiments possible in exploring the dimensions of the medium and what each stroke suggests in terms of application to subjects are almost endless. Your doodling will acquaint you with the possibilities faster than anything else and at the same time, put you at ease with your tools.

A size 12 round sable with little water and a fair amount of color was used for the dry brush stroke. Its use can be seen on the tree trunk and shack above. The vertical grass strokes below, were drawn in with the beveled handle of the Aquarelle brush while the color was still wet; those above were drawn using the brush as shown.

Avoid objects of equal size, similar shape, and texture.

Don't scatter the elements of your composition.

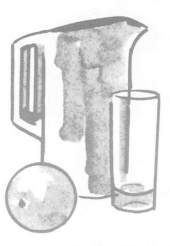

Vary the viewpoint, look down on the subject — move around it and examine all the possibilities.

Still life subjects offer an excellent opportunity for getting to understand the properties of watercolor as a medium.

The suggestions on these pages for arrangements apply to working in any medium, of course, but are important and worth repeating.

Start with simple objects that vary in size, shape, and texture. These will provide the most interesting possibilities for arrangement. Create interest and vitality in your grouping by contrasting light against dark, highly textured material against simple, smooth areas, etc. Visually frame your compositions with your hands, adding or subtracting items until your still life works as an interesting group in terms of arrangement as well as overall shape.

On the opposite page, can be seen some simple geometric possibilities for still life groupings. Variations on these such as an off center triangle, an oval, or a vertical rectangle can be used for many interesting arrangements that retain a compositional unity.

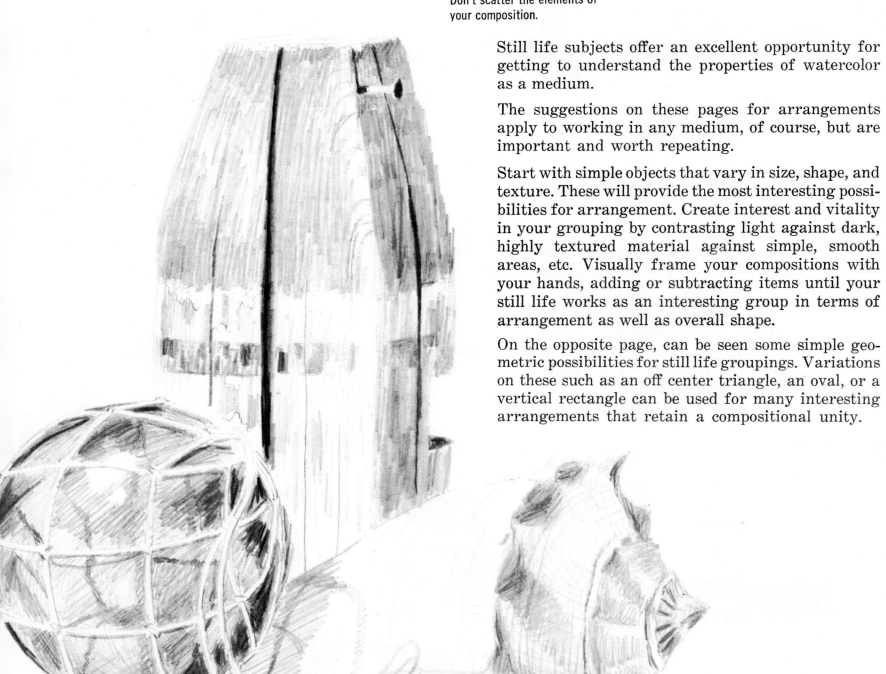

It is a good practice to make rough sketches of arrangements before starting to paint.

"Fruit and Wine" is a composition based on an off center triangle. The draped cloth spotlights the darker elements as well as acting as a foil for the play of textures in the principal elements.

I had previously stretched a sheet of 140 lb. Capri cold-pressed watercolor paper by soaking and taping it to a drawing board as shown on page 158. When dry, I penciled in the composition.

1. With the board flat, I flooded the surface and while still quite wet, used size 8, and 12 round sable brushes and a 1″ Aquarelle brush loaded with color to rapidly lay in the warm background. I used a combination of the colors from the subject, putting them in quite at random. These colors were: Cerulean Blue; Thalo Green; Burnt Sienna; Yellow Ochre; and Ivory Black. The Thalo Green was mixed with Yellow Ochre and Burnt Sienna for the warm earth green of the background.

2. While the background was still damp, the draped towel was painted allowing its edges to merge. A semi-dry sponge helps to control too much diffusion or "exploding" of color — simply pick up the excess with a sponge. Folds and shadow areas were brushed in while the paper was still damp. Next, the wine bottle was put in with washes of Thalo Green. Ivory Black was used for deep accents while the bottle area was still wet.

The remainder of the painting was finished by pre-wetting certain areas where necessary to soften edges. The sponge was used for these "second chance" softenings and blending of color.

If you find this too ambitious at the outset, you might try painting elements such as the pears and knife, apple, or bottle until you feel more confident.

The palette used was:
Cadmium Yellow, Pale
Grumbacher Red
Thalo Green
Cerulean Blue
Burnt Umber
Burnt Sienna
Yellow Ochre
Ivory Black
Payne's Gray

As a preliminary to painting, select a few flowers to draw in detail. It will give you a better grasp of the form involved.

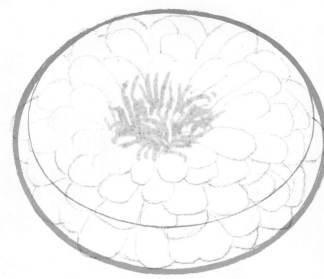

The Zinnia is contained in a circle or an ellipse. The area of the light pistils in the center of the flower is painted over with a masking material. Masking friskets can be made using either tape or fluid. They are applied to block out an area to keep it free from paint.

Flower painting, in addition to being excellent practice in the study of subtle color harmonies, broadens understanding and develops facility with the brush. The nature of the subject is such that much of the drawing and indication of form is done by the manner in which the strokes are put down.

Practice strokes for the indication of leaf, stem, and blossoms of various types. You will find that a great deal of what you want to paint can be done with single strokes if they are applied with confidence. More color on one side of the brush than the other will make for a stroke that suggests form and dimension beautifully.

When you are ready to try painting a flower arrangement, limit your penciling to the lightest possible indication of overall shape and direction. Keep your statements as direct and fresh as possible with the brush.

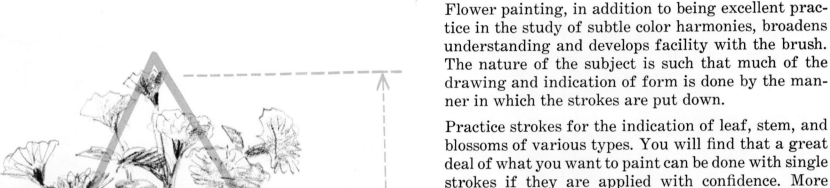
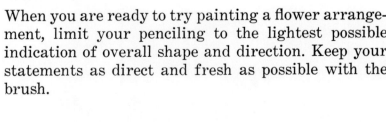

Group your arrangements within a shape. A good rule to follow is to keep the flowers 1½ to 2 times the height of the container. A matter of keeping emphasis on your subject.

While the first light wash is still wet, paint in the shadow side being careful not to come too high into the center. This same value is used to indicate the center depression.

Finish up by removing the masking material and a with a fine brush, define petals with darker cast shadows. The darkest accents should be saved for last.

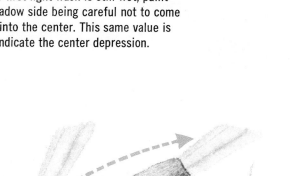

Start leaf painting as a light wash from the tip of the leaf — spreading the brush as you stroke.

While the leaf is still wet, put in the middle values and accent the edge with one slightly darker.

Pay particular attention to the manner in which leaves attach and flow out from the graceful curve of the stem.

Add cast shadows and veins. The highlights of the vein are scraped out with a razor blade.

These roses were so fresh and exciting as a subject in themselves that I felt it a mistake to have any indication of container in the painting — and chose instead to handle it as a loose vignette with the complementary green of the leaves as a foil for the color in the flowers.

A sheet of 140 lb. cold-pressed Arches watercolor paper was soaked and taped to a drawing board as in the previous demonstration. When the paper had dried, I lightly penciled in the elements of the composition I had chosen from my thumbnail roughs of various possibilities.

The brilliance of the subject demanded that I add additional color to the basic palette. For the cold red, I used Thalo Crimson and for the warm red orange, a mixture of Vermilion and Cadmium Yellow, Deep.

1. I re-soaked the paper using a sponge and while it was quite wet, I put in the warm red shapes with a size 8 brush and followed this immediately with the cool red.

2. The dark greens and middle value of the leaves were put in next — while the paper was still quite damp. Petal details were put in with a size 3 brush without attempting to delineate each one — too much detail in these would have overworked the painting and detracted from the overall wet-in-wet quality.

With another brush and clear water, edges were softened in spots and additional color accents added allowing a fusing of color in re-moistened spots. The final step when the paper was dry, was to touch up leaves with a few accents and indicate the stems.

The palette used was:
Cadmium Yellow, Deep
Vermilion
Thalo Crimson

Permanent Green, Light
Raw Umber

Before tackling a subject as ambitious as this, practice with individual blossoms. Moisten paper and lay in color at various intervals during the drying process of the paper to determine at what levels of dryness various effects are best achieved.

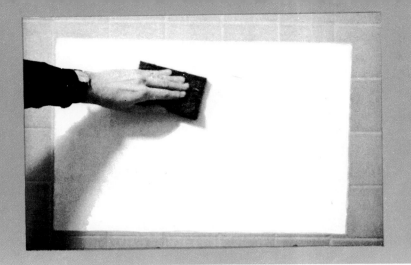

The following procedure is used stretching watercolor paper for painting. Usually it is not necessary to mount papers, 300 lb. and up.

1. Draw a line ¾ inch from the edge on all sides as a guide for putting on the tape.

2. Soak the paper in the bathtub or sink for 15 minutes or longer.

3. Cut strips of 1½ inch heavy gummed paper tape approximately equal to the length of the sides of the watercolor paper.

4. With a sponge (preferably synthetic because they do not break up), squeegee excess water from both sides of the paper. This can be done on the bathroom wall as shown.

5. Place paper on drawing board, plywood or pressed wood panel and lightly blot the edges to be taped.

6. Place the moistened tape along the line previously drawn, overlapping the paper and the surface of board. Sponge over the tape once it is in position. As the paper dries, it will stretch slightly and buckles will disappear. It should be dry enough to use in about an hour, depending upon weight of the paper and atmospheric conditions.

It is helpful to have the experience of observing and capturing nature first hand by painting on the spot. There is a vitality and quality to the roughest of outdoor sketches that often eludes more studied work.

For your outdoor trips, there are additional pieces of equipment you will find valuable. At the left is a photograph of what I usually carry on trips.

For paper, I use a 300 lb. (R) or (CP) which needs no stretching and can be tacked to a drawing board. On occasion I use the Capri Watercolor Block, which comes in a variety of sizes.

You can sit on the ground, but a collapsible easel and a folding stool allow you to work with greater ease and comfort. I also carry a large Capri Folding Palette for mixing paint.

The following items fit nicely into a zippered bag or knapsack: Collapsible canvas stool, mailing tube for carrying brushes, paint box and extra tubes of color in a box, two jars of water, one pocket knife, a box (with pencils, single edge razor blades, kneaded erasers, sandpaper pad, natural sponge, blotters and liquid frisket) sun glasses, bottle opener, plastic sheet (for rain), and lunch.

When you are painting outdoors, don't feel that you have to cover a sheet of paper completely and paint a picture every time you come to a subject that intrigues you. Making many quick, loose studies on the sketch block can be more helpful sometimes and equally as much fun.

The sketches on this page are some of the quick studies made on the spot for the painting on pages 16 and 17 which was done in the studio. I often take Polaroid or 35MM camera shots to be used for reference. The photographs in themselves are usually not enough without the notes to recall the excitement of the subject.

This winter scene was painted on an 18″ x 24″ Arches rough watercolor block using a palette limited to Yellow Ochre, Burnt Umber, and French Ultramarine Blue.

After penciling in, frisket was applied to the Birches. The paper was then wet down with the sponge. The sky was washed in with a mixture of all three colors but with the French Ultramarine Blue and Burnt Umber dominant. Next, the hills were put in using Burnt Umber and Yellow Ochre with just a touch of French Ultramarine Blue. The mass of trees above the snow was brushed in next with Burnt Umber. The tree trunks in this mass were painted in with a size 3 brush — fine branches were scratched out while the paint was still damp. After this, the shadows on the snow were put in with French Ultramarine Blue.

After the paper was dry, the frisket was removed and the figure and shadows on the Birches were painted. For the shadow on the trees a mixture of Yellow Ochre and French Ultramarine Blue was used, highlights were left unpainted. The distant patch of snow was covered with a light wash of the same mixture. A razor was then employed to scrape in the spray of snow behind the skier.

A liquid frisket was applied to block out the Poplar trees and fence for later painting. The sponge was employed for the sky and the foreground grass was scraped in with the tip of a knife blade while the color was still wet.

Masking tape was put over the mast and boom crutches. A liquid masking solution was used on the figures, sail, panels, and line at the back of the boat. A sponge was used for pre-soaking the paper. A razor blade was utilized for scraping out water highlights when the paint had dried.

The paper was wet with a sponge after the pistils of the tulips had been blocked out. Frisket was used on the string over the ball float before wetting the paper with the sponge. Highlights on the ball, cork, and sand were scraped out with a razor. A rag was employed to lighten the paint on the top front surface of the ball.

Transparent watercolor employs the white paper instead of opaque white paint for tints and white areas. The limited use of accessories to achieve these accents maintains the freshness and spontaneity of the painting.

SPONGE: Good for pre-wetting paper. Experiment with it for soft cloud effects. It is also useful for washing out paint for the re-painting of areas. (Synthetic sponge is more durable for vigorous squeegeeing but not as satisfactory for other uses.)

SINGLE EDGE RAZOR BLADE: Useful for scratching and scraping out small highlight accents as on water or small branches, and fine lines. It should be used after paint has dried.

POCKET KNIFE: A dull blade pressed through semi-wet paint will give you a secondary value in tree trunks and branches. Applying more pressure on the paper will produce wider strokes. When painting trees, re-wet spe-cific areas and try the knife for indicating branches in a deep color mass. The beveled handle of the Aquarelle brush can be used in a similar manner.

MASKING TAPE/LIQUID MASKING SOLUTION: Use tape on masts, poles, and simple straight edge masking. Liquid masking solution (frisket) is suitable for more complicated shapes. The masking material can be removed after the paint has dried. Any necessary form can be indicated in area previously blocked out.

RAGS AND BLOTTERS: These are a must, not only for cleaning and blotting but also for lightening painted areas.

ADDITIONAL IMPLEMENTS: Erasers, toothbrushes, stencil brushes, facial tissue, fingernails — in fact, anything handy that will assist in producing textural effects or patterns are useful. Just don't overdo the tricks.

Often a vignetted painting, with its soft uneven border, works well with contrasting geometric forms in the composition. In this painting, our view is led around the curve to the center of interest, a sunlit house.

The strong vertical of the pole counters the horizontal shape of the painting. Normally, the shadows are quite blue on a warm sunny day but I chose to keep them on the warm side to create to the feeling of warmth in the painting.

1. After lightly penciling in the subject, I used frisket on areas I wanted to keep white for painting later. (The frisket shows as a dark gray on step 1.) I wet the sky and tree area, to the edge of the roof tops. The sky color was washed in and while the area was still wet I put in the foliage at the top of the painting.

2. I continued in this manner, wetting specific areas and applying color. If an area wasn't too large, and did not require some wet-in-wet effect, the color was applied directly to the dry paper.

When the painting had been built up in this manner and each area covered, the razor was used for some final accents.

The painting was done on a Arches cold-pressed water-color block using the following palette:

Cerulean Blue	Cadmium Red, Light
Cobalt Blue	Hooker's Green, Light
Yellow Ochre	Burnt Umber
Cadmium Yellow, Pale	Payne's Gray

1

2

3

The abstract pattern studies on the left were made to show the pattern of the painting at the bottom of the page opposite. Number 3 shows the pattern involved in a second version of the same subject. This painting is shown on pages 168-169.

I started this painting of a Berkshire barn in the morning and had worked out the elements of the composition (Study 1 and 2) before starting to paint. This kind of preliminary study points up the basic forms. The play of hard edge against soft curves, the pattern of light and shadow, the strong horizontal planes with intersecting verticals, all become very evident and make possible adjustments which strengthen the composition and lead to a better painting.

Step A and the finished painting opposite were the first impressions. (Preliminary Studies 1 and 2) I arbitrarily moved the large Elm to have it bisect the dull right side of the barn and form was added to the left of the mountain for better balance and to create a visual flow into the line of the eaves.

As the afternoon light changed, it presented another possibility. By moving back to a lower point of view, placing the barn higher in the composition, and emphasizing the almost back lighted effect with the sun reflected on the shed roof, the subject became much more dramatic. Study 3 at the bottom of this page shows a rough preliminary sketch in black and white for the compositional possibilities of this second view.

The importance of exploring all the angles and possibilities of any subject cannot be overemphasized. Consider this as you walk around and familiarize yourself with what you are about to paint. Some material is so rich, you can paint it a dozen times or more.

Step B on the opposite page shows the preliminary lay in of color for the full color painting on pages 168-169.

A

B

Cadmium Yellow, Pale

Cadmium Orange

Alizarin Crimson

Hooker's Green, Deep

Cerulean Blue

French Ultramarine Blue

Payne's Gray

Yellow Ochre

Raw Umber

Burnt Umber

Note how the dark foreground trees break up the strong horizontal planes and act as a contrasting accent to the white roof of the shed.

1. The area of the sky was wet with clear water and a sponge and the pale clouds and distant line of trees were put in. The house and barn roof were painted next, followed by the entire barn which was laid in as a dark solid unit with Raw Umber to which Alizarin Crimson was added to this while it was still damp. The light grass areas behind and in front of the barn and house were painted next. Shadows were then brushed.

2. Foreground weeds were put in next using a 1″ Aquarelle brush and the shaped end of the handle was used for indicating texture of the grass while the color was still damp. Cerulean Blue used in the sky was repeated in the brook along with darker values produced by mixing French Ultramarine Blue and Hooker's Green, Deep.

The darkest trees were put in last. When the painting had dried, a razor was used to scratch out highlights in the water.

This painting was done on a Arches water color block 18″ x 24″, cold-pressed, using the palette shown on the left.

The manner in which you handle the sky in your landscape can be the difference between a successful painting and one that just misses. In many cases, you will find dramatic possibilities for treating certain subjects by making the sky the most dominant portion of the painting. Time should be spent in practice on a smaller scale before tackling the problem as part of a large painting.

Try indicating different types of clouds, the dramatic quality of the sky before a storm, the washed feeling after a storm, or the soft mist of early morning.

In the Vermont winter scene (#1 above), the clouds were painted wet-in-wet. For dark, heavy clouds such as this, French Ultramarine Blue or Payne's Gray with a touch of Burnt Umber is very good. Raw Umber might be used in place of the Burnt Umber for a slightly yellower cast to the clouds. Notice how the clouds flatten out as they recede. Sometimes a patch of Cerulean Blue sky in the distant background adds a dimension to the painting.

In #2 below, the sky is seen on a windy sunny summer day with billowy clouds. The low rolling bank of cumulus clouds with their undersides reflecting the sea and ground below them are moving rapidly. This necessitated painting quickly in wet-in-wet, tipping the paint-

ing to allow shadow colors on the bottom of the clouds to run into the upper portions. When the sky color was dry, I re-wet edges with a sponge to soften them in spots or to add more paint where necessary.

In #3 we have an illustration of cirrus clouds. Mix your color and plan your strokes before starting to paint. I painted this without pre-wetting the paper, working from dark to light in long streaks of color. A sponge and blotter are very helpful for keeping the washes under control.

A spring storm is extremely dramatic (#4). For this, put down a light wash of warm color, let it dry, and then re-wet sections and bring in explosions of cool dark

color for the cloud forms. Remember to flatten out the lower clouds as they reach the horizon.

Some of the most beautiful sunsets come right after an afternoon storm (#5). The clouds in this case were painted wet-in-wet in the upper portion of the sky with the board held fairly flat to control the running of the color from one area to another. The lower clouds were painted on paper quite dry.

Misty, moody skies are usually one soft graduated wash and distant hills should be put in while the paper is still quite wet (#6). Middle ground areas should also be kept somewhat undefined with hard edges limited to the foreground for contrast and depth.

This painting which concentrates primarily on the dramatic quality of the sky was executed on stretched 140 lb. Capri rough watercolor paper.

1. After very lightly penciling in the elements of the subject, I soaked the area of the sky down to the top of the distant hills, using a sponge. Cerulean Blue, as seen in the bright patch of open sky, was brushed in and around this I applied washes of Raw Umber allowing the colors to fuse. The Raw Umber was introduced toward the horizon as well. The middle value clouds were painted using French Ultramarine Blue mixed with Payne's Gray and the darker clouds primarily with Payne's Gray with much more pigment in the brush. The paper was quite wet through all of this and the Raw Umber underpainting fused into the blue and gray.

2. The next step was to paint in distant hills. For warm earth color accents, I used washes of Burnt Sienna and for the closer hills, Hooker's Green, Deep. In the larger hill form, French Ultramarine Blue mixed with Burnt Sienna was used. This area was moistened at spots where I wanted a soft blending with the sky. The board was tilted back to let color run into the sky area in a limited way.

The painting was finished using Hooker's Green, Deep, Yellow Ochre, and Burnt Sienna for the foreground. Light branches were scratched into the mass of the first line of trees using a pocket knife. Darkest accents were put in last and when the painting had dried, the roof tops of distant buildings, the road in the distance, and the bird above the trees were scratched out with a razor. The palette used on this painting was as follows:

Cerulean Blue   Raw Umber
French Ultramarine Blue   Burnt Sienna
Payne's Gray   Hooker's Green, Deep
Yellow Ochre

A

B

C

On these pages, we show the possibilities for viewing a subject and in addition, a few of the many ways in which the subject can be cropped or vignetted.

A photograph of the subject can be seen at the bottom of page 175 and above it an analysis of basic forms involved. By showing the photograph and the studies on these pages, we hope to demonstrate how much artistic license can and should be taken in the creation of a painting. The station is picturesque, but it is up to the artist to add, delete or change the position of poles, trees, branches, etc., and generally capture a mood that has a story telling quality.

D

E

F

A. In this study, the late afternoon sun highlights the front of the station. Strong horizontal shadows from the right counteract the diagonal lines of the track.

B. This is a September storm, a moody scene created by the dramatic aspect of the sky. Leaves and grass blowing give evidence of the wind. The building and horizon have been lowered to make the sky a more important part of the painting. A touch of white, blowing paper breaks up the solid gray mass and adds to the windy effect.

C. In this study, we see the building from the other side with the pattern of the crossing guard directing the eye. The weeds in the foreground help to suggest a quality of desolation.

D. Here, we see a more distant view with the bleak, abandoned quality accentuated by the wintry weather and the foreground weeds.

E. In this study, the first rays of morning light foretell a bright day. Add additional horizontal shadows to emphasize the low sun and create foreground interest.

F. The painting of the building has been increased in size to fill more of the picture. This approach was painted at noon on one of those sunny, cumulus-clouded days.

The atmosphere of complete loneliness in this painting, "End of the Line," was created by the damp, cloudy day; barren limbs; hanging wire; and the littered, wind swept landscape. The painting was done on a sheet of stretched 140 lb. Capri rough watercolor paper.
The palette used was as follows:

Cadmium Yellow, Pale	Hooker's Green, Deep
Yellow Ochre	Raw Umber
Alizarin Crimson	Burnt Umber
Cobalt Blue	Payne's Gray
French Ultramarine Blue	

After wetting the paper, the sky was washed in with a very thin wash of Cobalt Blue and in the cloud forms, a mixture of this same blue with Raw Umber and Alizarin Crimson was used. The distant trees were put in while the paper was still wet using varying mixtures of Hooker's Green, Deep and Raw Umber.

The station was blocked in with washes of Alizarin Crimson and on the shadow side, washes of Burnt Umber and French Ultramarine Blue were put over the original wash of Alizarin Crimson. The roof was put in with Raw Umber - French Ultramarine Blue mixed with it at the darker peak.

The painting was finished by putting in foreground grass with the Aquarelle brush, adding some grass strokes with the end of the brush handle. Additional strokes with changes in color with a size 3 brush when this had dried.

In approaching the problem of painting the "Tarry-town Light," shown on pages 180-181, I found that the subject lent itself to many moods and interpretations. I had passed this spot on a number of occasions, each time noting the effects of light and making quick pencil sketches for future reference. A sketch book carried with you at all times can be a great reminder for future trips, or source material for painting indoors in bad weather.

As a preliminary to painting, I made a number of compositional roughs, shown at the bottom of page 179.

In this rough, I felt the composition lacked the feeling of isolation that is so much a part of this subject.

The light structure against the dark sky in a vertical painting, offered dramatic possibilities but still lacked the isolated feeling.

The distant view of the dark mass against the sky and water seemed to offer the best possibilities for expressing this isolated feeling.

This painting was done on a sheet of stretched 140 lb. Capri rough watercolor paper. The palette used was as follows:

Yellow Ochre
Burnt Sienna
Alizarin Crimson
Cerulean Blue
French Ultramarine Blue
Sap Green
Payne's Gray

The paper was dampened, but allowed to dry quite a bit before applying a light wash (Cerulean Blue mixed with Yellow Ochre) very loosely to the upper portion of the sky. The white of the paper was left to indicate broken clouds. The lower portion of the sky was re-moistened and the wash continued to the horizon line. While this was still damp, I put in the line of distant hills using Sap Green and touches of Alizarin Crimson.

The lighthouse and the rock forms were next painted in using a mixture of Yellow Ochre, Sap Green, and a touch of Payne's Gray on the building and varying mixtures of Payne's Gray and Burnt Sienna on the rock forms. Alizarin Crimson was used with this mixture at the base of the lighthouse. Reflections in the water were done in washes of the colors used on the building with French Ultramarine accents brought into the lower portion.

Details on the building and rock mass; the flag; boat in the distance, and rowboat in front of the rocks were put in last. When the painting had dried, accents such as smoke from the boat funnel, edge of the rowboat, and the landing stairs were scratched in with the razor blade.

Donald F. Mo~~
TARRYTOWN LIGH~

ACRYLIC POLYMER

One of the most recent and most exciting developments in material for the artist has been the introduction of acrylic polymer paints.

These colors are particularly interesting because of the many techniques in which they can be used. They produce flexible, fast drying, paint films which are highly water resistant when thoroughly dry. Hyplar®, the acrylic polymer manufactured by M. Grumbacher, Inc. is available in a complete range of colors, and can be handled like transparent water colors in traditional wet-in-wet techniques. Since the colors are insoluble once dry, paper can be repeatedly soaked without the danger of original applications of color being affected. They can also be used as a gouche (tempera) and in a more impasto manner as with oils. The color can be built up without danger of chipping or cracking. Acrylic poly-

mer is an excellent underpainting for oil paints. A prepared Gesso, Modeling Paste, and a Gel (transparentizer) are also available.

The mediums, Gloss or Matte may be used to control the reflective properties of the surface of the painting, both as additives to the color or as final varnishes. The mediums also act as excellent binding agents for collage techniques or for additive materials in a painting such as sand, sawdust, cloth, paper, etc.

The palette of colors to start with can be the same as for oil. See the materials section page 4 or the basic palette listed on page 52.

Brushes, painting knives and other equipment associated with traditional media can be used with acrylics. i.e. Watercolor brushes and equipment when used as a

1

2

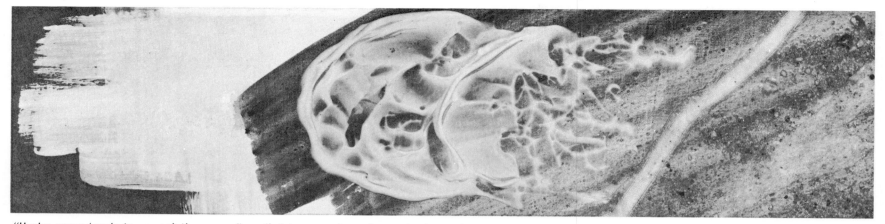

"Hyplar gesso (ready to use painting ground) applied to pressed wood can also be used as a ground on any non-oil surface.
Modeling Paste-extender can be mixed with color or applied as an underpainting for textures and impasto techniques.
The medium (matte or gloss) may be to bond materials to the painting for added textures — sand, wood chips, paper, cloth, etc.

watercolor and bristle brushes for oil techniques. Nylon bristle brushes especially made for acrylics make clean up a little easier. Colors should not be allowed to dry on the brushes.

To mix colors use a piece of glass, a polyethylene surface or a disposable strip palette. Because of the rapid drying put out on the palette only the color to be used immediately, rather than laying out a palette of color as with oils. Colors can be kept moist with an occasional spray of water from a hand atomizer.

When finished painting — brushes should be washed in soap and water.

At the bottom of page 182 (#1), the color is applied in a wet-in-wet technique. With acrylic polymer, much more control is possible with this technique than in traditional watercolor because the paper can be allowed to dry and then re-wet for subsequent washes without the danger of disturbing the original wash (#2).

When interesting "accidental" textural effects are called for in certain subjects — try blotting the color with a scrap of paper while still wet or by first putting the color on the paper scrap and then applying it to your painting as shown in #3. This can be glazed over for additional depth or textural effects without disturbing any of the previously painted area.

Acrylic polymer may be used as an opaque medium in which white is used to produce tints (#4).

3

4

In this painting "Winter on the Hudson" Donald Moss uses Hyplar as a transparent watercolor. This was painted on an Arches cold-pressed watercolor paper.

The order of painting was as follows:
1. After the basic drawing had been blocked in and paper dampened in the sky and cliff area, a single wash was put in and the upper line of trees indicated while this was still wet. Deeper values on the cliff were also put in while the paper was still wet, using a mixture of Raw Umber, Yellow Ochre, and Thalo Blue. Additional texture using the same mixture was put in with a dry brush when this area had dried.

2. The river color is a mixture of Raw Umber and Thalo Blue and the hull and window areas of the tug, Ultramarine Blue mixed with Raw Umber.
The foreground canvas covered boat, pilings, snow, other details against the cliff were painted last. The

razor was used for white accents and the ridge line of the cliff. All white areas in the painting are the white of the paper, no white paint was used with any of the colors.

The palette was: Yellow Ochre; Grumbacher Red; Raw Umber; Hooker's Green; Ultramarine Blue; Thalo Blue.

In the remaining demonstrations Christopher Davis demonstrates acrylic polymer as an opaque medium and in a very heavy impasto technique.

The peace and quiet of boatyards (the people around them are usually accustomed to artists) enables one to do careful studies of the abundance of material available. Spend this time gathering material for fruitful painting back at your studio. If time permits of course do as much painting on the spot as you can. The difficulty of transporting and setting up equipment limits this so that I find it much more desirable to make many quick sketches, color notes and roughs. I supplement these with studies done in whatever medium is easiest at the moment—pencil, felt pen or pen and ink. Occasionally, when the subject calls for it, a second color is used with the sketch to add all the value that is needed. At this point it should be mentioned that photographs are of great value but only as an aid to studies made of the subject. As a rule photographs alone cannot recall the mood and excitement which may have existed when the subject was viewed originally.

The felt pen drawing opposite — together with a rough color sketch was the basis for the painting on pages 188-189. In this case the texture and dark mass of dock and boats made the statement without regard to the infinite detail. This is not to say that detail isn't important, but for the student it can sometimes be a matter of not seeing the forest for the trees.

The mounted drawing paper (illustration board) was given a coat of Hyplar gesso over the entire surface because I desired a rougher texture.

1. A mixture of Cadmium Yellow, Deep and Cadmium Orange was painted over the entire surface. The drawing was then penciled in. The sky forms were developed using a palette knife and color applied quite liberally. Lighter values of the same colors, mixed with white, were brushed into the foreground; The mass of distant trees was put in with a mixture of Grumbacher Purple, Cadmium Orange and white.

2. The dark masses of the drawing were put in with Mars Black. A brush was used for the boats and dock and a small flexible painting knife for the grass in the foreground. Reflections in the water were a mixture of Grumbacher Purple and Burnt Sienna.

3. Color was then put in using a painting knife or brush depending on the amount of texture or detail called for. Most of the foreground was put in with the knife for the interesting textures the knife imparts.

The painting was finished by continuing in this manner. Color values in the dark massed areas were kept deeper than the darkest value of any of the light areas. In this manner the strong shapes of the dock, boats and grass kept their bold statement of a silhouette against the sky and water.

Many preliminary studies should be made before starting to paint rock forms.

A pressed wood panel was prepared as a painting surface by applying successive coats of Hyplar Gesso. The gesso should be dry between applications and it is best to brush the coats at right angles to each other (i.e. the first coat applied top to bottom vertically, the second, horizontally).

1. A tint of color, Thalo Blue, Thalo Green, Titanium White, with a touch of Grumbacher Purple was brushed over the entire surface. When this had dried the drawing was put in using black for the rock masses and white for the surge and direction of the wave. This simply establishes the drawing and is not necessarily what will remain as black or white in the final painting. With polymer one can work back and forth — changing and adjusting. This stage should be put in quite freely.

2. Starting with the middle values the progressively lighter and darker values were then put in; some with brush, some with palette knife depending on the texture desired. A wash of Grumbacher Purple and Thalo Blue was put over the rock forms which pulled them together as a unit while still allowing the black drawing to show. The palette knife was then used to lay in color on the rock as well as the wave forms. The original black and white over the background color acts as a guide to structure. It doesn't matter if it is somewhat obscured at this stage.

3. Working with the palette knife, additional texture was put in with Hyplar Modeling Paste mixed with color. Putting in, scraping out, painting over with the knife, until the desired texture or form was achieved. With polymer the fast drying permits re-working of areas light over dark, dark over light until you have exactly what you want.

In finishing the painting the last step was to re-state the lightest and darkest tones where necessary. The palette used was Titanium White, Cadmium Orange, Grumbacher Purple, Thalo Blue, Thalo Green, Burnt Sienna, Burnt Umber and Mars Black.